Facilitating Challenging Groups

Groups—like the people in them—come in all forms, and often they don't fit a standard mold. Single session, leaderless, and open groups are three of the most common kinds of nonstandard groups, but participants and facilitators of these kinds of groups have few, if any, resources at their disposal when they try to confront the unique challenges that their group structures present. *Facilitating Challenging Groups* confronts these challenges head on and offers activities, tools, tips, and techniques vital to everyone from the smallest self-help group to the largest human-relations training session. Readers will come away from this book with a deep understanding of each group's unique needs, the leader's role where applicable, and concrete strategies for developing the two traits most important to any successful group: universality and hope.

Nina W. Brown, EdD, is professor and eminent scholar of counseling at Old Dominion University. She is a fellow of the American Group Psychotherapy Association and the author of 23 books, including *Creative Activities for Group Therapy* and *Psychoeducational Groups*, 3rd edition.

Facilitating Challenging Groups

Leaderless, Open, and Single Session Groups

Nina W. Brown

Routledge
Taylor & Francis Group

NEW YORK AND LONDON

First published 2014
by Routledge
711 Third Avenue, New York, NY 10017

Simultaneously published in the UK
by Routledge
27 Church Road, Hove, East Sussex BN3 2FA

Routledge is an imprint of the Taylor & Francis Group, an informa business

Library of Congress Cataloging in Publication Data
Brown, Nina W.
　　Facilitating challenging groups : leaderless, open, and single session groups /
　　Nina W. Brown.
　　pages cm
　　Includes bibliographical references and index.
　　1. Group facilitation. 2. Social groups. 3. Self-help groups. I. Title.
　　HM751.B766 2013
　　305—dc23
　　2013011256

ISBN: 978-0-415-85714-7 (hbk)
ISBN: 978-0-415-85715-4 (pbk)
ISBN: 978-0-203-79866-9 (ebk)

Typeset in Utopia
by EvS Communication Networx, Inc.

SUSTAINABLE
FORESTRY
INITIATIVE

Certified Sourcing
www.sfiprogram.org
SFI-00555
The SFI label applies to the text stock.

Printed and bound in the United States of America by
Walsworth Publishing Company, Marceline, MO.

This book is dedicated to my grandchildren
Billy, Joey, Samantha, Christopher, Nick and Emma

Contents ● ● ● ● ●

Acknowledgments　• • • • •

Expressions of appreciation and thanks are extended to my professional organizations that continue to provide the most up-to-date information about groups; the American Group Psychotherapy Association, The Society of Group Psychology and Group Psychotherapy (APA Division 49), and The American Association of Group Work. Appreciation is also extended to the following individuals who contributed inspiration, and answered questions: Rebecca MacNair-Semands, Hylene Dublin, Molyn Leszcz, and my acquisitions editor, Anna Moore.

1

• • • • •

Facilitating Challenging Groups: Leaderless, Open, and Single Session Groups

The reality of leading a group can be very different from the leader's educational and training experiences. Group leaders can encounter many unanticipated and sometimes difficult events and situations with their groups. Many preparation courses and programs are geared to providing the knowledge, skills, and techniques for facilitating a particular type of group, usually a closed group with consistent membership and a limited number of sessions. The reality of practice may be that even when the group is closed, the leader is unprepared to cope effectively with sporadic or inconsistent attendance by one or more group members; a member terminating his or her participation without notice; life events for members that affect their ability to attend a group session; the leader's inability to screen out or terminate inappropriate members (e.g., for non-attendance) because of policies that are in place; and so on.

In addition, there is little information presented in preparation programs about leaderless, open, and single session groups. An examination of six textbooks and other leading books on group facilitation has shown that most do not present any information on leaderless and single session groups, and while all do have some information on open groups, that information is limited (Corey, 2008; Coyne, Crowill, & Newmeyer, 2008; Forsyth, 1999; Jacobs, Masson, & Harvill, 2009; Posthuma, 2002; Yalom & Leszcz, 2005). There are many of these challenging groups in the field, and this book is intended to fill these gaps. It is intended to provide guidance for entry-level and untrained group leaders who are called on to facilitate these challenging groups, and for trained group leaders who may be leading one or more of these groups for the first time.

Chapter 1 provides descriptions and definitions for three types of challenging groups, a rationale for some perceptual shifts leaders need to make, ethical considerations, and an overview of the remaining chapters. To get oriented, let's begin with defining and describing challenging groups.

● ● ● ● ●

Open Groups

Open groups are not easily defined but can be conceptualized as groups organized around a common theme or purpose, the duration for the group is open-ended, members are added or terminated along the life of the group on an as needed basis, and these groups call for a high level of leader flexibility to accommodate the ever changing group membership (Gruner, 1984). Examples of groups that fit this category include some support and self-help groups, some substance abuse treatment groups, and peer supervision groups for mental health professionals. Some of these examples will also be classified with the leaderless groups.

Other characteristics of open groups include the following:

■ The leader may be formally trained to lead groups, may be an untrained leader, or the group can be peer facilitated.
■ The emphasis may be problem/issue focused, or the group is used as a teaching tool, such as some training groups (T-groups).
■ The group is created as an open group.
■ The group may not have a definite life span, or can be time bound.
■ Some groups may have mandated membership (e.g., court ordered), while others have voluntary members.
■ Open groups call for a different set of leader skills and perceptions than do closed groups.
■ Progression or stage development differs from that found in closed groups described in the literature.
■ Ambiguity and uncertainty are continuous as new members are added and other members leave the group.

● ● ● ● ●

Leaderless Groups

Leaderless groups can be found in many venues, such as training groups for mental health professionals, self-help and support groups, and some treatment groups such as the long term leaderless women's group described by Counselman (1991) that has some therapy aspects. Leaderless groups usually do not have a professional leader or facilitator who is responsible for the group and its functioning, although when the group is composed of mental health professionals there can be one or more members who alternate responsibility for facilitating group sessions. The term *leaderless*, in this discussion, refers to the absence of a formal group leader who is not a group member but is responsible for the group's functioning. These groups have their own benefits, concerns, and challenges that revolve around or are associated with the lack of a formal leader. Some major characteristics for these groups are as follows:

- There is usually no designated leader/facilitator. Members assume this role.
- Some or many leader tasks are not fulfilled.
- The purpose for which the group was created can become lost or blurred over time.
- Group members who assume the role of leader are likely to be untrained in group leadership and consequently may not understand group dynamics and how to manage group leadership tasks.
- The group can be helpful for members' sharing, venting, and as a source of support.
- These groups may run the risk of "Group Think" that produces a situation where disagreement and differences are not tolerated.

● ● ● ● ●

Single Session

Two types of single sessions groups are discussed; the planned single session group, and the unplanned single session group. The planned single session group has a specified time frame where all members attend or are expected to attend the full session. Unplanned single session groups refer to planned multisession groups where one or more members will terminate prematurely, usually without notice, after the first session.

Single session groups are just what the title describes—one session. It can be frustrating to have to lead a group where the time constraints do not permit the learning, the dawning of awareness and insight, the unfolding of process and group development, or many of the group factors that have been shown to be helpful but that also need time to develop. Leaders can wonder about the usefulness of conducting a single session, but there can be also be positive outcomes when the leader understands the possibilities for effective use of the available time. Further, it may be that several sessions are planned, but one or more members attend a single session. The discussion will address how to make this limited participation positive for both the leader and the group member(s).

There is another use for a single session group perspective. It could be helpful to organize a multisession group so that each session is self-contained (Brown, 2011), so that even inconsistent attendance, such as what can happen when the group is open, allows members to receive some benefits from the sessions that they do attend.

Other characteristics of single session groups include the following:

- They may be planned as single sessions, or can be unplanned when the attendance contract is not honored and there is premature termination for one or more members.

- The leader may be trained in group leadership skills, but not prepared emotionally for members to attend only one session.

- There may not be screening or pregroup preparation for the group.

- Planned single session groups tend to be structured and theme focused, such as teaching performance appraisal techniques.

- It is difficult or impossible to establish a therapeutic relationship for unplanned single session groups.

- The unplanned single session may produce a negative impact on the leader's self-perception of self-efficacy.

● ● ● ● ●

Perceptual Shifts

The perceptual shifts that are needed for many group processes are very important for group leaders, especially trained group leaders, because these can differ for challenging groups as opposed to the usual closed group. For example, the planning process is a part of the preparation and training for group leaders (Corey, 2008; Yalom & Leszcz, 2005). This planning process will be very different for some challenging groups, however, and while some planning is recommended for all types of groups, some leaderless and self-help groups may not use it because of the lack of a trained leader, or because of leader absence or leader turnover. The trained group leader may need to make some perceptual shifts, but an untrained or temporary leader can benefit from knowing what and how these processes work for the particular type of group.

Chapter 2 presents an overview of general group processes and procedures as they are related to groups overall, but the literature that supports the use and efficacy of these is primarily based on findings from long- and short-term closed groups. Thus, these need to be perceived somewhat differently when applied to open, leaderless, and single session groups. It can be somewhat disconcerting to be the leader of one of these types of challenging groups and to unexpectedly realize that the usual group processes and procedures either do not apply to the current group, or have to be applied in a different way only after the group begins. The perceptual shifts needed for each type are presented in the sections on the particular type of group.

There are also some personal perceptions that may be held by group leaders and need modification, especially those that relate to conventional social behaviors and attitudes, but are not helpful for the group and members in a therapeutic group setting. Social attitudes and behaviors include the following:

- The leader expects that he or she is supposed to make members comfortable and works to make this happen instead of understanding that it is more helpful if the group leader can tolerate some of their discomfort because this can be where growth, insight, development, and healing can take place.

- The leader constantly works to soothe members' uncomfortable feelings rather than allowing them to take responsibility for self-care.

- The leader overly explains in an effort to try and eliminate ambiguity and uncertainty which tends to promote more questions and concerns. It is more helpful to discuss member feelings that emerge about ambiguity and uncertainty as this can reduce the anxiety they may have.

- The leader asks questions as a means to encourage members to tell the entire story with all of the details instead of focusing on the member's perceptions, understanding, and feelings about the relationship(s) being discussed.

There are also some internal attitudes, perceptions, and feelings that can be counterproductive for the group leader:

- The leader has a strong desire to "fix it" and make it better for members rather than having faith in the group and its members' competencies and potential to fix it for themselves.

- The leader expects that he or she is supposed to have and give the group the "right" or perfect response every time. It is acceptable to be able to provide a good enough response most of the time.

- The leader takes responsibility for members' feelings instead of allowing members to take responsibility for their own feelings.

- The leader reacts to comments and remarks from group members as being personally critical or blaming. It is much more helpful when the leader can engage in self-reflection about the feelings and other reactions aroused in him or her because this allows the monitoring of countertransference.

- The leader is very fearful of making a mistake, which in itself prevents him or her from having the courage to take an appropriate risk. Thus, the leader will miss out on the learning that can ensue. Risk taking can prevent some empathic failures.

- A strong desire on the part of the leader to be approved of by members to the point where this is a major concern, and some group needs, such as conflict and confrontation, are suppressed, denied, or ignored. It is much more helpful when the group leader focuses on and addresses group and members' needs in spite of the discomfort this presents for the him or her.

- The leader may expect dramatic breakthroughs and be disappointed when these do not occur instead of emphasizing the importance of members' incremental steps toward growth, development, and healing and recognizing them when they take place.

- The leader may perceive tears and crying as weaknesses versus considering them as expressions of intense feelings, such as pain, frustration, joy, or relief.

● ● ● ● ●

Ethical Concerns

Group leaders who are trained mental health professionals usually have professional organizational ethical standards or a code that they are expected to honor, and, if licensed, there are also state professional standards and ethical rules that must be obeyed. Untrained group leaders and those who are not mental health professionals do not have these formal institutionalized rules, but nonetheless they are expected to behavior ethically. This presentation is intended to serve as a reminder for both trained and untrained group leaders of some basic and fundamental ethical issues that can be applied and followed: confidentiality, documentation and reporting, scope of practice, and duty to warn.

Do No Harm

Dimidjian and Hollon (2010) define treatment harm as being symptoms that are caused by the treatment and were not a part of the presenting problem. Examples of treatment harm include when the client's or group member's improvement slows; the therapist or group leader causes distress that is intense and enduring, not just temporary and worked through; the treatment provided is not helpful; there is the use of potentially harmful treatment interventions as identified by Lilienfeld (2007); the presenting problem becomes worse; and there is cost to the client of the unhelpful treatment.

While the course of improvement can have highs and lows, when improvement slows after being steady and consistent, that can signal that the treatment has become ineffective, which is defined as being harmful. The group leader has an obligation to be aware of the deceleration so as to institute more effective treatment(s) for a particular group member or members.

Group leaders can expect that members will experience or encounter distress during the group sessions. However, when that distress is not noticed, is ignored, or not attended to, then members can leave the session with those distressing feelings having become mired or overwhelming, and this situation can be difficult or impossible for them to manage on their own, which in itself is harmful. The distress is theirs, and may have many reasons, but the group leader is causing harm by not recognizing the distress and working to moderate or eliminate it so that the member can manage any residual feelings outside of the group.

Group leaders try to select treatment strategies and techniques designed to help group members reach their treatment goals, but when the strategies or techniques are ineffective, those goals become unattainable. It is not unusual for a strategy or technique to be ineffective at times, even when it is one that usually produces positive results. However, persisting with an ineffective strategy or technique can lead to harm for the client or group member or members. Group leaders have a responsibility to assess the outcomes of their selected strategies and techniques and, when these are being ineffective for the particular person or group, to cease using them and to find more effective ones.

Lilienfeld (2007) reviewed randomized controlled trials, quasi-experimental studies, meta-analyses, and naturalistic studies to create the list of potentially harmful treatments, and thus these are empirically supported. The treatments on the list had to meet certain criteria: harmful physical or psychological effects were shown for the client or for others; the harmful effects persisted over time and were enduring; and the studies and findings were replicated.

Harmful treatment effects were described by Lilienfeld (2007) and Boisvert and Faust (2006) as follows:

■ The treatment procedures and processes produce deterioration for the client.

■ The client does not improve with treatment.

■ The client's relatives or friends are harmed by his or her responses to treatment.

■ Premature termination occurs as the client cannot tolerate the treatment.

■ The presenting problem, symptoms, conditions, and the like become worse with treatment.

■ New symptoms appear after treatment is begun.

■ The client expresses anxiety and concern about the course of treatment and his or her rate of improvement.

■ Physical harm results from treatment.

Even when the presenting problem is not the "real" or underlying one, it can be harmful for that person when the problem brought to the group becomes worse, such as a member becoming more anxious, depressed, angry, and so on. Group leaders are helpful when they can set collaborative goals with the group and with individual members, work toward these goals, and monitor progress toward achieving them. This too can prevent failure to notice that the presenting problem has become worse or has started to worsen.

There are many costs associated with treatment even when group members do not have to pay money for the treatment. Their costs also include time; costs for arriving at the site such as for transportation; costs for child care for some members, as well as the emotional investment and other intangible costs. These costs are also born by members whose treatment is not paid for by insurance for one reason or another, but who pay directly. Thus, when treatment is unhelpful or harmful, there is the additional burden of the costs of treatment for group members.

Prevention of Potentially Harmful Treatment (PHT) for Challenging Groups

Prevention strategies that can help reduce or eliminate the possibility of group leaders using potentially harmful treatment (PHT) can be derived from the literature on effective group leader tasks and strategies. Examples include enhancing the therapeutic relationship (Horvath & Bedi, 2002; Martin, Garske, & Davis, 2000); the leader's knowledge and understanding of how the therapist contributes to negative interactions, ruptures in the therapeutic alliance, and his or her influences and impact on improving therapeutic outcomes (Binder & Strupp, 1997; Castonguay et al., 2004); continual monitoring and managing countertransference (Gelso & Hays, 2007); the ability to identify transference without analyzing it (Crits-Christoph, Gibbons, & Connolly, 2002); and a recognition that the best predictor of outcomes is the level of the therapist's developed self (Wampold, 2006).

Confidentiality

Confidentiality is a major concern for many group members who fear that the personal material they disclose will be revealed to others outside of the group, and some can even fear that their attendance at the group will be revealed and this will result in possible negative consequences for them. Group leaders will find it is a good practice to not talk about their group members with others unless, such as in the case of supervision, they can do so in a general way so that the member cannot be identified. Further, group leaders will find it helpful to openly discuss members' fears and concerns about confidentiality, the limits on what the leader can keep confidential, the lack of leader control over what members may knowingly or inadvertently reveal to others outside of the group, and guidelines for what can be shared with others who are not in the group.

Some leader responsibilities and limits on confidentiality can include court-ordered reporting, sharing information with other treatment professionals, disclosures to third-party payers, when there may be danger to a member or to others, and an inability to control what others may do or say. It can be essential for group leaders to remember that group members have to consent in order for the leader to share information, even with other treatment professionals, and their written consent must be obtained at the outset before any information is shared.

- If there is a need to share information with other treatment professionals, tell group members what the limits are for maintaining confidentiality under these circumstances, and the purpose for sharing information.

- When there are court-ordered disclosures to be made, these should be specified in advance, conveyed and understood by all parties concerned, and be as narrowly defined as possible. In all cases, the group leader has the responsibility to try and limit the amount of information to be disclosed to others, and to restrict it to essential information.

- In the case of third-party payers, such as insurance companies, the same restrictions for court-ordered disclosures also apply, with the added restriction that the group member, or a parent or guardian, must authorize the release of information in writing when possible.

- There is an ethical responsibility to report when a group member exhibits clear and eminent danger to self or others, and when there is a contagious life threatening disease. Group leaders are also advised to be aware of and follow federal, state, local, and institutional laws and policies for reporting on these conditions.

Other ethical responsibilities that are related to confidentiality are the members' culture, privacy needs, and an inability to be of help. It is important for the leader to understand members' cultural context for maintaining confidentiality. Some conditions and illnesses are considered shameful in some cultures, and there is a stigma attached to these conditions or illnesses. Leaders should not assume that members have the same cultural context as they do. Maintain a respect for members' privacy, especially about some personal matters that can be gender or age related.

What may seem unimportant to some people and to the leader may be very shame inducing for others. When leaders find that they cannot assist group members for any reason, such as lack of proper training, significant countertransference issues, personal illnesses, or crises, it is their ethical responsibility to provide appropriate referral or other transfer of services. Finally, it is essential that security be maintained when sharing or transmitting information about group members to anyone outside of the group. This means that the leader does not share any information about the group or its members in public places, such as hallways or lunch rooms, and that leaders remain aware that there may be a lack of security for both cell phones and land lines, fax, e-mail, or voice mail, and take proper precautions when using these means of communication.

It is also important for group leaders to discuss the expectations and limits for confidentiality. Whereas the leader can affirm that he or she will maintain confidentiality, the leader cannot provide the same assurances for other group members. If there is an expectation that group members are to maintain confidentiality, and this is an essential expectation and rule to have, the leader cannot guarantee that this will be the case. Further, there can be laws or policies that mandate the leader to break confidentiality. Please consult your state laws, professional standards, agency, or institutional policies for this vital information, and notify group members of these limits for maintaining confidentiality.

Group leaders will want to be cautious and circumspect, and to educate group members to be the same, with what they discuss with group members outside of the group, especially with a member who disclosed some important personal information in the group. For example, a member may have disclosed information about a personally distressing situation, and you want to check in with him or her to provide encouragement, support, or as a caring gesture. However, it could be that when you ask about it outside of the group, others can overhear, or worse, just asking could arouse that person's distressing feelings. While you may not have disclosed any details or particulars, just asking about it could be revealing to others and a violation of confidentiality. It is suggested that check-ins outside of the group be made in general terms, such as "How are things going for you?" This question is general enough to not reveal that there is anything specific you are inquiring about, and is also a socially conventional question.

Group members may be tapped into the use of social media, such as Facebook, Twitter, and the like, and are so accustomed to posting personal information that they may not think to censor what they communicate about the group. Group leaders are advised to have a discussion about what information can and cannot be posted, and to provide the guidelines in writing. Appropriate topics for posting can be personal thoughts, feelings and ideas, and major topics discussed, such as conflict resolution. Inappropriate topics include any personal disclosures by members or the leader, members' names or other identifying information, or even when and where the group is meeting. Any information that should be kept confidential is not appropriate for posting or sharing with others.

Documentation

Documentation can also cause concerns about confidentiality, and required documentation such as case notes should be discussed with group members; examples of these would include reports to others regarding court-mandated group members or to insurance companies that require reports or other documentation in relation to claims. There are also legal restrictions for what can be reported, and requirements for group members' signed permission for release of information. There are additional requirements that relate to group members who are not considered adults under state or federal laws. Leaders working in institutions such as agencies, hospitals, schools, and the like should be familiar with the requirements for documentation and reporting.

Scope of Practice

Scope of practice refers to conducting groups within the extent and level of the leader's knowledge and expertise which, for licensed professionals, can include academic training and supervised practice. Professional standards and ethical codes usually caution against the use of techniques and strategies for which formal academic training and supervised practice are lacking. Group leaders for the types of challenging groups described in this book must be aware of the need to have the academic and formal knowledge and supervised practice for the techniques and strategies they propose to use with their groups.

Overview of the Book

The book covers issues that relate to general information about groups; leaderless groups; open groups; single session groups; and group activities. Each area will be covered by several chapters that include illustrative activities and techniques.

General Information

The first chapters address fundamentals of group leadership as applied to the three categories of group: open, leaderless, and single session. Chapter 1 introduces definitions for challenging groups, needed perceptual shifts for leader attitudes and behaviors, and some major ethical concerns. Chapter 2 focuses on general group factors that include basic information about group dynamics, stages of group development, and Yalom's (1995) therapeutic group factors. Chapter 3 presents the framework for developing a therapeutic alliance to include the related attributes and communication styles for group leaders, developing the therapeutic alliance, the importance of the leader's emotional presence, empathic responding, and the identification of empathic failures and empathic failure repair.

Open Groups

The chapters on open groups focus on the challenges for this whole area. Chapter 4 defines and describes open groups and challenges and the potential benefits. Chapter 5 describes the issues, concerns, and some possible helpful strategies for planning open groups. Chapter 6 presents facilitative skills, techniques, and specialized activities for open groups.

Leaderless Groups

The chapters in this category include descriptions of the various types of leaderless groups and a literature review regarding their outcomes. Described are suggestions for structure, direction, and facilitation. Central to the success for these groups are clearly stated goals, purpose, and procedures; rules, and the availability of one or more group professionals for consultation or supervision. Chapter 7 presents descriptions for different leaderless groups and the literature available for self-help, support, and other types of leaderless groups, and the benefits and constraints. Chapter 8 presents guidelines that address leadership/facilitative strategies, member behaviors both challenging and facilitative, rules for engagement, realistic expectations and assessment for these, and group members' safety measures.

The Single Session Group

The chapters on the single session groups discuss the challenges that group leaders encounter with both planned and unplanned groups. The major challenges for the leader are that many times growth and development cannot unfold and be observed, there can be an air of futility in even trying to accomplish something positive, and other such constraints and limitations. Chapter 9 describes single session groups, the benefits that can be gained, and the constraints for both the leader and the members. Chapter 10 focuses on planned and unplanned single session groups with information on premature termination, and how to manage this. The self-development of the group leader is emphasized in addition to the knowledge and skills that person will need when facilitating these groups. In addition, the value and use of self-contained sessions for multisession groups will be presented, especially those that may have inconsistent member attendance. Topics covered include establishing trust and safety, setting realistic collaborative group and individual goals, encouraging the emergence of therapeutic factors such as hope and interpersonal learning, and strategies for building group members' awareness to help them capitalize on their strengths.

Activities

The final three chapters present activities that can be used in one or more of these types of groups. Activities presented in earlier chapters tend to be applicable for the particular type of group under discussion, while those that follow in the final two chapters will be more generally useful.

Chapter 11 focuses on activities for getting started such as ice breakers and introductions, presents a rationale for using them, and describes how these activities can help the group and its members. Chapter 12 presents activities focused on building members' self-esteem and self-confidence and emphasizes a focus on strengths. Also presented are activities for encouraging and supporting members in expressing their emotions. Chapter 13 focuses on the importance of clear communication, conflict resolution, and closure.

2

• • • • •

General Group Factors

Group leaders will find it helpful to understand the importance of the stages of group development, how to identify group dynamics and their impact on members and on the group, group therapeutic factors as described by Yalom and Leszcz (2005), group process, managing conflict, and problem member behaviors. These are the usual topics covered in group leader preparation programs and training, and the literature supports their importance for the group (Strupp, 2001).

• • • • •

Group Stages

Different theorists and authors present some variations in how they conceptualize the stages of group development, but there is general agreement that many groups do move through some stages. Understanding these stages allows the group leader to identify members' progress, capitalize on the dynamics taking place at any particular time in the sessions, and provides clues for interventions.

Tuckman (1965) was among the first to propose and document developmental sequences for groups, and this later became known as group stages. These stages are not separate, distinct, or easily identified. Tuckman titled them as *forming*, *storming*, *norming*, and *performing* (1965).

Other terms and descriptions include the following:

- Engagement, differentiate, individuation, intimacy, mutuality, and termination (MacKenzie, 1990);

- Orientation, conflict, cohesion, stability, and termination (Yalom, 1995);

- Formation, conflict, rebellion, and termination (Weber, 2000);

- Formative, reactive, mature, and termination (Rutan & Stone, 2001);

- Defining and structuring procedures; conforming to procedures and getting acquainted; recognizing mutuality and building trust; rebelling and differentiating; committing to and taking ownership; functioning maturely and productively; and terminating (Johnson & Johnson, 2006);

- Beginning (1), conflict (2), cohesion (3), and termination (4) (Brown, 2011).

It can be difficult for group leaders to immediately identify the group's stage of development in closed groups, except for stage 1 where the group is forming, because the transition from one stage to another is gradual, or there can be regression to an earlier stage, and characteristic behaviors that are associated with a particular stage can emerge in other stages. For example, harmony is associated with the performing or cohesion stage where members are open, authentic, and provide feedback to each other. They identify and work on important issues and concerns. However, there can be periods or parts of sessions where this behavior appears when the group is in other stages. The difference would be that, if the group were in stage 3 (cohesion), this would be the most consistent behavior among group members, and not just an occasional event.

It can be even more difficult to identify the group stage for the challenging groups, and for the untrained group leader. The untrained leader may not be aware of the rich source of information to be derived from understanding group members' behavior during the various stages. For example, the second stage of group development is usually characterized by conflict among group members and attacks on the leader. Both of these can produce considerable discomfort and may trigger feelings of inadequacy and incompetency for the group leader because the behavior can be apparently unexpected. The same feelings and reactions can also appear for the trained group leader, but can be more easily dissipated when the leader remembers that the behavior is characteristic of this stage of development, and can work to help guide members to understand and work through their conflicts.

● ● ● ● ●

Group Dynamics

As was the case with group development stages, group dynamics also have different perspectives.

- Forsyth (1999) defines group dynamics as being both a field of study and group processes.

- Lewin (1951) defined group dynamics as the powerful processes that take place in group.

- Johnson and Johnson (2006) note that the field of group dynamics is a "twentieth-century, North American development" (p. 35) that derived its origins from many fields and has evolved into an interdisciplinary field.

- Brown (2009) proposes that contemporary emphases for group dynamics focus on the continuous movement and progression of the group, and on the interacting forces that impact the group and its functioning.

Bion (1961) introduced the idea of the group as a whole, and this work added greatly to the understanding of how the whole group functioned. Bion proposed three basic assumptions for groups; dependency where members feel helpless and look to the leader for support; fight/flight where the group feels in danger and uses one of these actions as a response; and pairing where members have hopeful fantasies of being saved and of the group being constructive.

While group dynamics are defined in different ways, they are always present, ever moving and changing, and exert influence on the group and on its members. For example, resistance is always present for the individual group members who may or may not be aware of it, and resistance is also present for the group as a whole.

Observation and understanding of the group's dynamics reveal the current process for the group, and the identification and understanding of these dynamics allow the group leader to better intervene, and to help the group accomplish its task. Some basic group dynamics to observe as they unfold in the session include the following:

- Suppressed or denied conflict;

- What the group wants or needs that is unrecognized by them or is not being openly verbalized;

- The quality and level of members' participation and the relationships among group members;

- Clues to what is being resisted, such as intimacy, conflict, or challenging the leader;

- Understanding members' behavior and relationships outside the group;

- If a collaborative group secret exists;

- Cliques and subgroups;

- When or if members are being excluded;

- The potential for scapegoating to occur;
- Repressed or suppressed intense feelings;
- When and how to intervene.

Examples of some dynamics and their cues include these: *Level of participation* demonstrates the characteristic interaction style and behavior; and changes in interactions, input, and responses for individual members and for the group as a whole. *Verbal communication patterns* can illustrate if members are being included or excluded, if deference is shown to some members, where the members perceive the power and influence to be in the group, the unspoken group norms, and members' current emotional states. *Nonverbal behavior* carries valuable information about what the group and its members are experiencing at a deep level. Behaviors such as, voice tone, body positioning, facial expression, body movements or lack of movement, and clusters of gestures all convey deep and important messages about current emotional states for both individual members and for the group as a whole. How and what *feelings are expressed* can be an indicator of overt or hidden issues in the group, as well as indicators for individual members' emotional state, sensitivities, and resistance. Hidden, disguised, and suppressed feelings are important and significant for group members and for the group as a whole.

Resistance is an indicator of sensitive material for the members and for the group as a whole that is threatening and thus, must be defended against, suppressed, or repressed. Members can manifest resistance in different ways such as denial, deflection, intellectualization, and displacement. Conflict, either suppressed or visible, can also be an indicator of the group's fear, need, or wishes, as well as that for individuals, and the most important point to observe and understand is how the group manages conflict, such as denial, suppression, ignoring, and working to resolve conflict.

● ● ● ● ●

Group Therapeutic Factors

Yalom and Leszcz (2005) present group processes for which there is some evidence that they support promotion of growth, development, and healing (Kivlighan, Coleman, & Anderson, 2000; Kivlighan & Holmes, 2004; Kivlighan, & Mulligan, 1988). These factors are:

- Universality: commonalties among group members, such as values, experiences, reactions, and the like;

- Instillation of hope: realistic expectations for relief, coping, and functioning;
- Altruism: giving to others, such as providing encouragement, support, and the like;
- Imitative behavior: modeling effective relating and communications;
- Catharsis: expressing difficult and often intense emotions with an intrapersonal learning result;
- Group cohesion: the group is productive with members working on relevant concerns and demonstrating trust, caring, and concern for each other;
- Dissemination of information: providing education or training;
- The corrective emotional experience: members experience old feelings or thoughts, and receive positive reactions from group members that differ from past reactions by others;
- Interpersonal learning: giving and receiving constructive feedback;
- Socializing techniques: learning more effective ways to build relationships and communicate;
- Existential factors: becoming aware that human conditions, such as suffering, death, freedom, and will are universal, can only have answers for the present, and will recur throughout one's life. Reduction of feelings of isolation and alienation.

Some of these will naturally emerge, such as dissemination of information. Others do emerge but may not be used effectively, such as the interpersonal learning loop described by Yalom and Leszcz (2005). This can be the case especially for untrained group leaders who lack knowledge about the positive influence and impact on the group and on its members. Trained group leaders who facilitate open and single session groups can foster the emergence of some or all of these factors and capitalize on them. A discussion of these factors, how to recognize when they emerge in the group, and how to use these to benefit the group and its members are discussed in those chapters. A briefer discussion is provided for leaderless groups to describe how some can be identified.

● ● ● ● ●

The Planning Process

Planning the group and planning individual sessions can be very helpful even when the course of the group may not be predictable, attendance may be inconsistent, and members have different needs and agendas.

The groups that are the focus for this book can be especially difficult to plan, but even with those difficulties, some planning is highly recommended both for the entire life of the group and for individual sessions. In the case of planned single session groups, the planning would incorporate segments or sections for the one session.

Some benefits for planning are the following:

■ Planning provides some structure, which can help members feel safe and that they will be cared for.

■ Planning gives direction and focus for accomplishing the group's and individual members' goals and objectives.

■ Planning allows the group leader to understand what preliminary tasks need to be accomplished, such as gathering materials for activities.

■ Planning enables the leader to assess the viability of several alternatives for the group or for sessions and make a more informed selection.

■ Planning enables the leader to leave time for research and to search for strategies to fit the group and its needs.

■ When there is a teaching-learning component for the group's focus and emphasis, or even for a session or segment, planning enables the leader to select from several alternatives for presenting information, such as media, lecture, discussion, and so on.

■ Leaders can be more confident that the group or session has the tools to help ensure that progress can be made.

A process for planning is presented for each challenging group in the section that addresses that type of group.

● ● ● ● ●

Screening and Pregroup Orientation

Screening potential group members for suitability for the group can prevent many problems (Gans & Alonso, 1998; Yalom & Leszcz, 2005). However, this may not be possible for some challenging groups, such as self-help groups or those where members are compelled to attend. The screening process can also provide an opportunity for pregroup orientation where potential group members can receive information, set personal goals, and ask questions that can help reduce some of the ambiguity and uncertainty about what is expected of them, and discuss what the group can do to help them.

It is helpful for the group leader to develop a list of topics and questions for screening in order to assess the person's commitment to the idea of the group, verbal communication skills, interactive and interpersonal skills, what they imagine the group will be like, and even some of the fears or apprehensions they may have about the leader and other group members. Having such a discussion beforehand can allow the group leader to decide if the member is appropriate for the planned group, or if there is another option that would be better for that person. However, it is not always possible to screen members prior to the group; nor can the leader necessarily screen out a member even when there is ample evidence that the planned group is not appropriate for that person.

Pregroup orientation is also a helpful process where prospective group members have opportunities to explore their feelings about the group, and to receive information. Pregroup orientation can address the following topics:

- Expectations members have about what the group procedures and process entail;
- Dissemination of factual information about techniques the leader will use;
- Basic rules that cover the behaviors expected;
- A discussion of helpful behaviors that will help them with their growth, development, and healing, such as speaking of the thoughts, feelings, and ideas they have while in the group;
- Concerns about confidentiality;
- Collaborative goal setting;
- Leader qualifications and competencies.

● ● ● ● ●

Basic Group Rules

Group rules help to provide some sense of safety and trust for group members indicating that they will be cared for, and that the group will not get out of control. Following are some suggested basic rules that group leaders and members can adjust and add to:

1. Members are expected to attend each session on time, and to notify the group leader in advance when they are not attending, are unable to attend, or will be unavoidably late.
2. Members must treat other members and the leader with respect. Differences of opinion and the like are to be tolerated.
3. There must be no verbal or physical violence, and no weapons.

4. Members who are under the influence of drugs or alcohol will not be allowed to stay in the session.
5. Phones and other communication devices must be turned off.
6. Confidentiality must be maintained (see the discussion in chapter 1 for specifics).
7. Recording of sessions by members is prohibited.

● ● ● ● ●

Process and Process Commentary

Process is defined here as the present-centered interactions among group members and with the leader (Brown, 2003a). It incorporates what the group is doing, avoiding, ignoring, or denying, especially when these actions are inactions and are negatively affecting the group's functioning and progress. Tuning into process involves a focus and understanding of the group as a whole. While attending to individual members is important, the group entity also provides an understanding of what the individual members may not be aware of, or are not verbalizing. Process is not an easy concept to grasp and use because of its complexity, and can be especially difficult to recognize during a session where much is happening. The ability to tune into process is an advanced group leadership skill but can be significantly helpful for understanding the group's unspoken or unrecognized fears, hopes, wishes, needs, and the like, as well as those of individual group members. Because of its complexity, process may not be understood or used effectively.

Tuning into the group's process in a session requires the leader to understand and integrate the following elements with an emphasis on the entire group:

■ Usual member behaviors for the various stages of group development.
■ An understanding of how the metaphors used by members can be reflective of what the group as a whole is experiencing or longing for.
■ The session's theme to that point.
■ What the group as a whole appears to be resisting and how that resistance is being exhibited.
■ A deep understanding of the leader's objective countertransference and how what he or she is feeling could be the result of containing and managing members' feelings.
■ An awareness of the group's behaviors and dynamics for the session and what these may be reflecting that is unspoken.
■ An ability to sort through the myriad of feelings members are expressing and suppressing to focus on those that seem to have the most

important impact and influence for the individual members, and how these are shared by other members.

Process commentary is the act of verbalizing the leader's understanding of the group's process as an intervention. It's a way of holding up a mirror to the group so that all can see and understand what the group as a whole is doing or not doing, wanting, needing, and fearing, and how the actions or inactions of members are a reflection of these. Here is an example:

> *The previous group session was very productive with members doing considerable work. Members seemed to be making meaningful connections with each other. However, this session is very different with the members being irritable, cranky, and making snippy comments. The leader comments that the group is acting to prevent the connections established in the last session from becoming stronger, and it may be that the group fears intimacy.*

Process commentary is best done after the group has developed trust and safety among group members and with the leader because it can be very threatening to some group members who will receive it as criticism that they are wrong or not meeting expectations, which can be shaming for them. Group members need to have had enough contact with the leader to be assured that the leader has their best interest in mind, can be trusted to not inflict damage or harm, and is intervening with this commentary as a means to help guide the group and its members in productive work. It is for these reasons that providing process commentary may not be advisable for many of the groups that are the focus for this book, where there is insufficient time to develop the levels of trust and safety that are needed, and where inconsistent member attendance does not allow the group to coalesce and become cohesive enough for process commentary to be accepted. It is for these reasons that guidance for providing process commentary will not be presented for those sections, but recognizing group process will be addressed for all types of groups.

● ● ● ● ●

Managing Conflict

Conflict is almost always present in some form in a group, and how it is managed by the group and by the leader will determine if it can be a constructive or destructive factor for the group and its members. Differences of opinion, values, and perceptions are examples of conflicts, as are disagreements and clashes, but do not have to be or become battles where anger is expressed in hurtful and inappropriate ways. Differences can be expected, and members can be taught to respect and tolerate these.

Disagreements are likely to arise and members can be taught to express their diverse opinions and feelings so that they can be worked through and thereby strengthen relationships. It is when conflict in the group is suppressed, repressed, denied, ignored, minimized, or discounted that it can exert a negative impact on the group's process and progress.

In addition to members' perceptions and management of conflict, the group leader's reactions play an important role. For example, when a group leader fears conflict emerging in the group, that leader may take conscious or unconscious steps to keep conflict from emerging by ignoring, dismissing, or minimizing any hint of possible conflict. The possible positive outcomes for constructive conflict resolution are outweighed by the leader's discomfort or fear of even a mild version of conflict emerging in the group. The reasons for group leaders' perspectives of conflict can be varied but are usually associated with or related to family of origin experiences, or past experiences in nonfamily contexts where conflict was not only uncomfortable but destructive. Whatever the reason or perspective, the group leader still plays a major role in the management of conflict in and for the group.

Trained group leaders should have some knowledge and expertise in managing conflict and in teaching members how to engage in constructive resolution of conflict. Some untrained group leaders may also have the knowledge and expertise and this is very helpful for the groups that they lead. The absence of a formal or trained group leader can present a group situation where no one has the knowledge, expertise, or responsibility for managing group conflict, which can produce considerable discomfort, be damaging to some group members, and even cause some members to drop out of the group. Conflict management for some challenging groups can be a major constraint or barrier because of these groups' unique characteristics.

● ● ● ● ●

Problem Member Behaviors

Social convention plays an important role in group members' and some group leaders' reluctance and inability to intervene effectively with some common members behaviors such as storytelling, monopolizing, prolonged silence or withdrawal, ignoring group rules, constant complaining, and advice giving. Many group members and leaders who do not want to do or say anything that is rude, tactless, or offensive can think that it is their responsibility to ensure everyone's comfort and that others do not experience discomfort. It is for these reasons that many problem behaviors are allowed to continue even when it is evident that these behaviors are negatively affecting the group. Leaders can even encourage some of these problem behaviors with their responses in addition to not intervening to stop or block them.

Problem Behavior	Possible Motives	Encouragers
Storytelling	Need for others to fully understand his or her perspective;	Asking questions; Asking for details
Monopolizing	Need to prevent silence; Self-absorption; Desperately seeking answers or help but unable to recognize it	Listening without interrupting; Responding with advice, sympathy
Silence/withdrawal	Fear of being shamed, such as revealing a secret or the real self; Fear of rejection; Resistance to joining the group	Ignoring the person
Ignoring group rules	Self-absorption, such as an entitlement attitude; Need for power or control; Challenging authority	Ignoring such incidences
Constant complaining	Need for attention; Resistance to exploring the "real problem or issue"; Seeking sympathy Being a martyr; Wanting others to take care of him or her; Fear of inadequacy	Asking for details; Sympathizing; Agreeing that he or she is "right"; Giving advice; Trying to "fix it"
Advice-giving	Feel overly responsible for others; A desire to be helpful and to "fix it"; Need to be seen as superior and competent; Challenge to the leader's expertise and competence	Asking for advice; Seem to be accepting of the advice; Giving advice; Admiring of those who have the answers

As you can see, there are many reasons for these problem behaviors and when the group's life span is short, such as with single session groups, or attendance is inconsistent, such as with an open group, or when there are untrained group leaders, such as what can happen with some leaderless groups, or with any of the other types of challenging groups, there may not be sufficient time or expertise available to effectively address these behaviors or to prevent them from negatively affecting the group.

When problem behaviors emerge, it is the group leader's responsibility to address these, and to do so in a way that respects the member who is exhibiting the behaviors and the other group members. However, it is not an easy task to address these issues because it is not helpful to blame, criticize, put members on the hot seat, or "call someone out," because the member(s) can then become angry, shamed, guilty, or resistant. Further, other group members may also have negative reactions such as fear that the same will happen to them. The group leader is best advised to not ignore the problem behaviors, or to take the member aside to talk with him or her outside of the group in the mistaken belief that it is polite to do so. Talking with members outside of the group can arouse all kinds of fears and fantasies for the other group members, such as the thought that those members are getting the leader's attention, and the other members are not.

Best practice is for the leader to address the behaviors in the group in a sensitive manner because this will provide an opportunity to:

- Provide a corrective emotional experience where the person is not treated as they may have been in a previous relationship, such as the parental relationship;
- Demonstrate a constructive confrontation technique that has the potential to show how this can strengthen a relationship;
- Allow the leader to see the impact of the confrontation on other group members;
- Members will see that the leader will uphold the group contract or rules, and this can produce feelings of safety and trust.

Thus, the group leader has to balance the needs and emotional states of the member(s) exhibiting the problem behavior(s), the needs and impact of the intervention or absence of one on the other members and on the group as a whole, and the necessity for an intervention. The task then is to decide what to do and how best to do it. Following are some intervention strategies for the various problem behaviors, and a general script.

Storytelling

The group can be thankful for someone to work on, to take the lead in presenting their issue, and to keep the silence and tension from building. However, the details of the story are not the important points, nor can the leader and other group members know anything except that person's side of the story or his or her perspective. The most important points will be the feelings the storyteller has about the situation, and these can be solicited without asking for or needing details. When the person has gone into details, the story is becoming circular, and members are asking for details, the leader can intervene and block those questions by interjecting something like, "I think it will be more helpful if we can get a sense of the feelings you experienced or are experiencing." The storytelling will be curtailed by keeping the focus and discussions on the speaker's and listeners' feelings.

Monopolizing

The monopolizer is difficult to stop, and some group leaders are reluctant to intervene because of the social convention against interrupting someone who is speaking. In some cases, the person is trying to fill silences, is oblivious to the impact of the behavior on others, is very self-absorbed and feels that his or her concerns are more important than those of others. To intervene, the leader can also interrupt the speaker, and say something like this: "You've given us a lot of material to consider and I think it could be helpful to hear the thoughts, feelings, and ideas that emerge for other group members as they listen to you." Keep the focus on these as they relate to the issue the monopolizer is bringing to the group.

Silent-Withdrawn

The silent-withdrawn member can be fearful and resistant. Some people are very quiet, saying little most of the time. However, this becomes a problem when people in this category do not provide input or speak about their feelings in the present, or they say that they want to sit back and observe. This behavior can arouse anger in other members who can feel that they are putting their selves and issues out in the group, and want to work on these but feel that they are reluctant to if others will not do the same. An intervention that may work is for the group leader to say something like, "(Call the person's name) I'd really like to hear your thoughts and feelings about the topic. What's coming up for you as you listen to what was said?" Keep the focus on current feelings in the session, and not on whether or not the person in question has had similar experiences, which is irrelevant.

Ignoring Rules

Ignoring group rules is very serious because doing so can cause some members to feel that the group is not safe and that they will not be cared for. The group rules help define the group boundaries, and thus breaking rules means that the boundaries are breached. Leaders should avoid telling the offender that the rules say thus and so. It is better to start by noting the behavior, such as chronic tardiness, where the leader can tell the member that the group doesn't seem complete when all members are not present, and when a group member is late you don't know if he or she is going to attend or not. The sequence is to specify the behavior, and reaffirm the offender's place, role, or importance to the group; and to suggest a solution, such as notifying the leader when you will not attend or will be late given in the example.

Constant Complaining

What can be most helpful for the constant complainer is to try and understand the underlying anxiety, which is not easy to do. People who are persistent complainers can be trying to find a way to manage their anxiety, especially about distressing life events, perceived self-efficacy, and fear of rejection. Whatever the reason, the source of the anxiety may not be known to that person who may not be able to adequately express his or her concerns, and so turn to complaining about even minor things.

3

●●●●●

Developing a Therapeutic Alliance: Leader–Member Relationships

All challenging groups do not have a therapeutic goal or objective where the leader's alliance or relationship with group members is essential for successful treatment outcomes. This lack of an objective will influence the extent to which members will self-disclose and work on their concerns and issues and allow their vulnerabilities to be seen by others. Holmes and Kivlighan (2000) identify the relationship component that is most important for the group as emotional awareness because this produces insight and problem definition changes for individual members. Horvath and Bedi (2002) and Norcross (2002) found that the therapeutic relationship was a consistent predictor of positive clinical outcomes, and meta-analyses by Horvath and Symonds (1991), Karver, Jandelsman, Fields, and Bickman (2006), Martin, Garske, and Davis (2000), and Shirk and Karver (2003) provide additional evidence for the efficacy and importance of this relationship for positive changes, and group outcomes.

●●●●●

Description

The therapeutic relationship or alliance is defined and describe in different ways, but all seem to include collaboration between the leader and member, the member's confidence in the leader, an agreement on the goals for the experience, and trust in the leader's competence (Ardito & Rahellino, 2011; Rogers, 1979). Components include the following.

- Empathy, unconditional positive regard, and congruence on the part of the leader (Rogers, 1951);
- A reality-based collaboration (Greenson, 1965);

- The leader's understanding of the member's various attachment styles and needs (Bowlby, 1988);
- The member's perception of the therapist's competence (Strong, 1968);
- Agreement on goals of treatment, agreement on tasks, development of a bond with reciprocal positive feelings (Bordin, 1979; Horvath & Luborsky, 1993).

This relationship can make the difference between a group that is cohesive and productive and the group that is not. There are two primary aspects to consider for establishing the needed relationship: the leader's personal characteristics that define relating attributes, and the leader's actions.

● ● ● ● ●

The Leader's Personal Characteristics

Personal characteristics refer to the psychological inner resources, values, attitudes, and the developed self of the individual. These cannot be taught or learned as would academic material, but are a result of the interaction of the person's personality, temperament, self-understanding, and internalization of life's experiences. These are what determine the individual's ability to be caring, warm, tolerant, and respectful; the extent to which others are viewed as unique, valued, and worthwhile individuals; the capacity to be empathic, to have a rich and varied range of emotions, and reduced self-absorption. Achieving this inner development can be a lifelong process, and it is a worthwhile endeavor which can be very rewarding, especially for relationships both in and out of the group. It may be helpful to readers to describe and illustrate the characteristics and their roles in establishing a therapeutic relationship.

The core relating attributes for the group leader are defined as follows:

Caring—The ability to authentically value the client and a desire to promote his or her welfare.

Warmth—The nonverbal transmission of an inner state that is welcoming toward the other person, and that makes a meaningful connection with him or her. An example of this would be having a pleasant facial expression, initiating eye contact, and smiling when members enter the room.

Tolerance and respect—These terms refer to recognizing and accepting differences with others and not judging the person's differences as wrong, inferior, or a sign of personal inadequacy. An example of these would be the ability to accept other perspectives and values without saying or feeling that the other person is flawed.

Perceiving others as unique, valued, and worthwhile individuals— Indicates an absence of stereotyping and bias and an ability to understand where you end and others begin; in other words, a recognition of others as separate from oneself. An illustration of this is when you don't jump to conclusions about someone when meeting them for the first time.

*The capacity to be empathic—*Calls for an understanding of oneself as separate and distinct from others so that the act of being empathic allows you to enter the world of the other person and feel what he or she is feeling without losing the sense of yourself as being separate and distinct from that person. You neither become enmeshed nor overwhelmed by the other person's emotions.

*Having a rich and varied range of emotions—*Allows the person to have a deep emotional life, and the ability to express these emotions is important and helpful in the group. This characteristic models recognizing and expressing different levels of emotions from mild emotions such as irritation, to intense ones such as pleasure and fear.

*Reduced self-absorption—*Allows the group leader to be emotionally present in sessions, to monitor his or her countertransference, to tolerate greater levels of ambiguity, uncertainty, and conflict; to recognize and cope with members' transference and projections; and to be empathic.

These personal relating characteristics help not only to establish a therapeutic relationship, but also promote the development of trust and safety in the group with the leader and among group members. The major task is to be able to convey these positive personal characteristics to group members who are likely to be in crisis, or have past relationships where their trust was violated, or to have unresolved family of origin issues that make them tentative, cautious, and wary of trusting others.

● ● ● ● ●

Roles for Personal Characteristics

These relating characteristics have the following major and important roles to play in the group in addition to helping to establish trust as safety:

■ Acceptance of members as they are at the current time;

■ Promotion of the feeling of inclusion for members;

- Reduction of members' feelings of isolation or alienation;
- Conveying a nonjudgmental attitude;
- Giving encouragement and support;
- Modeling constructive ways to improve and strengthen relationships.

Acceptance of members requires a belief and attitude that each member is worthwhile, is doing his or her best to cope at this time, and each has realized and unrealized strengths. A major role in helping members to feel accepted in the group is played by the extent to which the leader conveys caring, warmth, respect, tolerance, and a nonevaluative attitude.

The leader has a significant role and the responsibility to promote the inclusion of all members in the group because this helps to develop trust and safety in the beginning of the group, and is a major contributor to the development of group cohesion. Trust is essential for members' willingness to self-disclose important and probably distressing feelings; to give and receive feedback; assist them in making meaningful connections; enable them to confront and be confronted; to work through conflicts in an effort to resolve these; and to encourage them to experiment with new behaviors. Feeling excluded can lessen or eliminate a member's commitment to the group, diminish the development of trust that the leader can or will take care of him or her, and other such negative responses.

It is not unusual for some group members to arrive in the group carrying feelings of isolation and alienation, and the leader and the group members can either help ameliorate these feelings, or by their actions reinforce them. The nature of challenging groups and the personal characteristics and development of the individuals who form the group can cause it to be more difficult to reduce these feelings. The following are leader tasks that can help reduce feelings of isolation and alienation:

- Help members understand that others have similar issues and concerns as they do (universality).
- Help members to see that others cope and get better (modeling or imitative behavior).
- Demonstrate to members that they can provide encouragement, support, and other forms of help to others (altruism).
- Provide opportunities for members to express feelings (catharsis).
- Help members to gain an understanding that existential issues, such as feeling isolated and alienated, are a part of everyone's life, that answers are only for the present, and that these issues will reemerge throughout one's life (existential factors).

- Guide members to become aware of their unrealized inner resources.
- Provide a group environment of acceptance, inclusion, and empathy.

The group leader who is able to establish and foster these elements is setting the stage for the group's success and group members' growth, development, and healing.

Group leaders and group members have opinions and values of what constitutes right and wrong, and good and bad behavior and attitudes, as well as holding evaluations about other aspects of people such as their worth and value as unique individuals. All of us are acculturated from birth through our families, and through the community and aspects of the larger culture to form these conscious and unconscious evaluations and judgments. Because of these experiences, it can be very difficult to be consciously nonjudgmental about others that we meet, and may be even more difficult to do for the group that we attend or lead. However, if the group and the members are to work on important personal issues and concerns, the group leader must display a nonjudgmental attitude toward group members. This is not to say at all that the leader has to agree or approve of the members' behavior or attitude, or to adopt them, it simply means that the leader does not openly say or convey an attitude toward members that is intended to be critical or blaming. For example, a member who discloses something shaming for him or her is helped more when the leader can listen and reflect the member's feelings than when the leader responds with a moral judgment about what was disclosed.

Both group members and the leader can provide encouragement and support, and the establishment of the therapeutic alliance can be facilitated when these are an integral part of the group's climate and norms. But, it can be the leader's task to note and comment on incremental improvements that members make as encouragement and support for them to continue doing what is working, or to applaud the efforts extended to making changes. Having faith in others' capacities and abilities can be affirming for them, increase their willingness to persist in the face of barriers, constraints, and other unanticipated events, and thereby help them to be successful.

Encouragement does not mean pushing someone to do something you think would be helpful for the person. Encouragement can come from the following leader's actions:

- Noticing and applauding small improvements especially if the person has yet to recognize these.
- Pointing out actions that the person took to reach his or her goal.
- Telling the person about his or her unrecognized strengths.

■ Redirecting or reframing negative self-thoughts the person verbalizes or demonstrates through his or her actions.

Support has many of the same positive outcomes as does encouragement. Support is not advice, it affirms the other person's ability to cope and manage even when there are missteps. It recognizes efforts made whether those are successful or not. Support is a foundation that illustrates your caring, positive regard, and valuing of that person.

The value of having meaningful, enduring, and satisfying relationships should not be underestimated, and the group can be a means of showing members how to initiate and maintain these. Members' relationships with each other and with the leader provide opportunities to teach and learn more constructive ways to relate and communicate through modeling by the leader, the leader's fostering of relating and communicating for members, and in some cases, by directly teaching them even when this is not the main focus for the group.

● ● ● ● ●

Leader Actions

There are some leader actions that can help to establish and maintain the therapeutic relationship:

■ An emotional presence

■ Listening and appropriate responding

■ Empathy and empathic responding

■ Soliciting members' input

■ Enforcing group rules and the group contract

■ Preparing the group environment

■ Understanding resistance

■ Repairing empathic failures

■ Working to resolve conflicts

■ Intervening to prevent attacks or scapegoating

An emotional presence means that the leader brings his or her thoughts, feelings, and ideas to the present so as to be more fully engaged with the group and its members. The leader is not thinking about his or her own personal issues or concerns, is actively listening to what is said by group members, and is observing group dynamics so as to provide any needed interventions. This emotional presence conveys to the members that the leader considers them as important, worthwhile, and is interested in them and in their concerns and issues. Behaviors that indicate real attention are suggestive of the leader's emotional presence to the members, such as initiating and maintaining eye contact, orienting one's body toward the speaker, having a pleasant and welcoming facial expression, and listening without interrupting.

Listening and appropriate responding are also valuable leader actions. Hearing the feelings and the content of verbal communications and providing an appropriate response promotes a feeling of being understood for group members. The feelings underlying the message, whether openly verbalized or not, can be the most important part of the message, but many people do not openly verbalize these or may not be able to access them. However, these conditions do not lessen their importance. The content is also important, but the feelings behind the content indicate the level of the importance of both for the speaker. Listening for both content and feelings gives the leader clues for an appropriate response even when the content may appear on the surface to be trivial or of little importance.

An appropriate response begins with giving a verbal response that acknowledges that the speaker was heard, and a more in-depth response takes it further and lets the speaker know that the message was understood. Appropriate responses avoid the following:

- Asking for more details or encouraging storytelling;
- Minimizing the speaker's emotional intensity;
- Ignoring the speaker;
- Changing the subject before acknowledging the speaker's message;
- Telling a joke;
- Providing a sarcastic response;
- Dismissing the message as being trivial.

Appropriate group leader responses include paraphrasing what was said to ensure that the speaker meant to say what was heard and that it was correctly understood by the listener; giving a response that reflects the speaker's content and the feelings he or she has about the content whether spoken or not; and empathic responses.

Paraphrasing involves restating the message in different words that capture what was meant and heard. This restatement does not change the content and intent of the message; rather, it reflects both elements without using the same words as those used by the speaker. Paraphrasing helps the speaker to know that what the receivers heard was what the speaker meant to say. For example, this can be very important when the speaker is emotionally intense and may not accurately communicate his or her thoughts, feelings, or ideas.

Reflective responses incorporate the speaker's content and feelings at a thoughtful and cognitive level that does not require the receiver to feel what the speaker is feeling as would be the case for empathic responding. The receiver understands what the speaker means and feels, but does so at a distance and is more detached. This response allows the receiver to know that the message was received and understood. The reflective response is a valuable technique for the group leader.

Empathic responding is invaluable as a basic and fundamental therapeutic tool (Brown, 2011; Rogers, 1951; Rutan & Stone, 2001; Yalom & Leszcz, 2005). It is not sufficient by itself, but it sets the foundation for therapeutic work by assuring group members that they are heard and that their feelings are understood at a very deep level. Empathy is more than what was previously described for reflective responses as it adds an emotional connection between the sender and receiver that is lacking for reflective responding. Empathy allows the receiver, for example the group leader, to enter the world of the sender, such as a group member, and to hear the content as well as feeling what the sender is feeling without the receiver losing the sense of him- or herself as a separate, distinctly different individual; and conveying those feelings to the sender. The receiver does not become enmeshed or overwhelmed by the sender's feelings, and does not substitute nonverbal gestures for a verbal response that clearly identifies the sender's feelings.

Soliciting members' input is another leader task. Some quiet members can need an invitation to contribute and the group leader can extend the invitation. This can be particularly useful when there is an emotionally intense topic that emerges in the group so that all members receive an opportunity to speak of their responses, thoughts, and feelings. It could also be the case that some members need permission to speak, especially about their feelings, because doing so has been discouraged in their past experiences. A group leader has to be alert and aware of members who may need encouragement or be directly asked for their input.

Rules are important for the group's safety and functioning. These are the expectations for all members, and it is extremely important that the leader take care to enforce these equitably and fairly. The rules provide the framework for members' behavior so it can be easily seen by all when the rules are broken or are not enforced. It's even worse when the leader ignores some members' breaking rules but enforces the same rules for other group members. This inequity can arouse concerns about fair treatment, trigger unresolved family of origin issues, or allow previous experiences of unfair treatment to reemerge, and thus affect those members' feelings about the group or the group leader, and which may also negatively impact their participation.

Preparing the group environment includes assuring that the space for the session is ready, there is adequate seating, lights, and a comfortable physical climate, that the environment is free from distractions, interruptions, or intrusions from outside the group, and that there are adequate and sufficient resources or materials if needed for the group's activities. It is also helpful when the leader arrives early to the session to check on the environment and to arrange the group circle even when this requires moving furniture. It is highly recommended that the group not meet around tables, even a sofa or cocktail table, and that seating be formed in a circle. This arrangement reduces physical barriers between members and with the leader, and can encourage interactions.

Resistance can be expected in all groups and the group leader needs to anticipate this and be emotionally prepared to recognize and deal with it, and to accommodate it in its many manifestations, covert and overt, such as the following:

- An abrupt change of behavior or the topic;
- Becoming defensive;
- Monopolizing, talking a lot;
- Remaining silent or withdrawn;
- Going on the offensive and attacking;
- Asking lots of questions;
- Challenging others instead of reporting on current feelings;
- An open refusal to provide input, report on feelings, and other such behaviors;
- Discussions that ramble, go nowhere, or are circular;
- Gossip and complaints that are not the central focus for the group;
- Becoming confused;
- Insertion of humor, inappropriate jokes, sarcasm, and other such responses;
- Becoming bored or expressing boredom.

The list of resistant thoughts, behaviors, and attitudes is very long. However, the main tasks for the group leader are to recognize resistance and then to leave it alone. It is more helpful to the group, especially in the beginning stages and for the challenging groups described in this book, that the leader not confront, push to resolve, or try to break down resistance, and that he or she block other members' efforts to do these. The resistance is there to protect the individual from perceived danger, either from external forces such as the group or the leader, or from internal forces such as fear, guilt, or shame. The resistance can be help-ful to the leader to help identify areas of sensitivity, but it is best to allow the person to decide when the danger has passed, or to realize that the danger is imaginary, or that they feel safe enough to trust other group members and the leader so that the resistance is no longer necessary. This process can take time; members need to establish sufficient con-tact with other group members and the leader to develop the necessary trust, and sufficient time is not necessarily available for some challeng-ing groups.

Empathic failures occur in therapy and can happen in all groups, and it is the group leader's responsibility to recognize and repair these (Brown, 2009; Kohut, 1977; Rutan & Stone, 2001). The failure to receive an empathic response can be very wounding and humiliating, and can trig-ger feelings of rejection, unimportance, exclusion, and anger. Examples of empathic failures include the following:

- A member makes an emotionally intense disclosure and no one responds;
- A member tells of an abusive experience but in the telling has little affect, and the group ignores it and changes the topic;
- Thinly disguised issues are ignored;
- Members or the leader zone out during the session;
- A disclosure is termed or thought to be trivial;
- Responding with a personal story instead of a direct and empathic response to the speaker;
- Use of humor or sarcasm to deflect or avoid emotionally intense disclosures;
- Interrupting the speaker and changing the topic.

Although the empathically failed group member may deny any feel-ings about the failure, it can still have an impact. The person will deny an impact or not be aware of its impact because of feeling ashamed of feeling rejected or ignored, consider what he or she was saying as incon-sequential, repress any negative thoughts or feelings, fail to recognize or want to recognize what happened or how he or she feels, or other such responses. The other possible outcome is the impact on other group members who observe the empathic failure, and who on some level can fear that the same could happen to them. Group leaders have a respon-sibility to recognize and initiate a repair of these failures in the group.

Conflicts, from mild disagreements to extensive clashes, are inevitable in the group, and, when they emerge in these challenging groups described in this book, could be harmful to some members or the group if not managed in a constructive manner. Group leaders are expected to recognize conflicts at all levels, to manage their countertransference to these, and to guide the group in constructive conflict resolution. This can be especially important to help members manage the group developmental stage where conflict is expected, to promote and strengthen relationships among group members and with the leader, and to teach them ways to manage conflicts in their out-of-group relationships. However, all of this takes time, knowledge, and expertise that may be lacking for many challenging groups.

Group leaders have the major responsibility to prevent or to intervene when attacks, scapegoating, or other problematic behaviors occur in sessions. One difficulty can be the leader's understanding of the potential and warning signs so as to intervene before negative impacts become destructive. While members and the group as a whole may be able to tolerate some discomfort when encountering these behaviors, too much discomfort produces distress which can have destructive and lasting effects on the group and on some group members. Even knowledgeable and experienced group leaders make errors in judging whether an exchange could be a fruitful exploration, or if it has the elements of an attack, will escalate if not interrupted, or has the potential to arouse considerable distress for those in the exchange or for other group members who are not directly involved. Then too, there can be individual members' perceptions about an exchange or other behaviors. While some members do not consider the event as an attack, there are other members who will perceive it as such.

Scapegoating is similar to attacks, but differs in that it is not an exchange between two members, but tends to occur when several group members address a perceived problem, or one member's unsatisfactory behavior. It occurs when the group has an unaware and unspoken issue or concern and deflects or suppresses it with an intense focus on one member who is judged by them to be an unsatisfactory member. While the overt focus may have some validity, such as addressing a member's continual silence, the underlying purpose can be to keep attention away from other members' personal issues or concerns, or as an unconscious or nonconscious collaborative decision to deflect attention away from an uncomfortable group need, such as a challenge to the leader. Hence, all of this is put on the unsatisfactory member for him or her to carry as the scapegoat for the group.

Examples of member behaviors that seem to attract becoming scapegoated are the following:

- Continual silence, lack of input;
- Verbalizing that he or she either doesn't have problems, or that others' problems are more deserving of the group's time and attention;

- Monopolizing, storytelling;
- Advice giving, having the answer;
- A superior attitude;
- Constant complaints about the same matter with no resolution;
- Asking for help but rejecting members' efforts as insufficient or not "right";
- Being closed off, combative, or argumentative;
- Always or constantly rushing to soothe others;
- Seeming to give cognitive responses but not feeling ones;
- Saying that he or she hasn't had a particular experience so cannot relate to the member(s) who did have the experience.

Attacking or scapegoating behaviors are difficult to illustrate, but there are some behaviors that have the potential to be or to be perceived as such. Examples of these behaviors include a barrage of questions directed to one member, members pushing for an answer or for input, challenging a perspective or opinion without first verbalizing empathy or an understanding of the other person's perspective, projected or displaced anger or fear or shame toward one or two members, and expressions of dissatisfaction with a member's participation or perceived attitude. Questions are helpful when there is a lack of information that is needed for an understanding of perspective or feelings. However, questions to gain more detail about a situation, event, or person do not provide material to help understand the other person's experience. Rhetorical questions, how or why questions, or questions that are disguised ways of telling someone what they should or ought to do or think are not helpful and the leader must block these. In addition, some members can feel attacked when they are asked many questions.

Another behavior that can be an attack or scapegoating is when members are pushed to provide an answer, or they have input, especially when this comes from several members in the same session. Inviting input or asking for a perspective is different in that an invitation should be extended in a manner that would also accept a refusal to provide these.

It is not unusual for members to have and verbalize opinions and values that are not shared by other group members and for disagreements to arise about these. However, when members challenge each other's opinions, with an attitude that the other person is wrong, misguided, or shameful, that can be received as an attack, no matter how mild the challenge may be, unless the challenger first verbalizes an understanding of the other person's perspective that includes both the content and their feelings. It is very easy to feel attacked and misunderstood when one's opinions and values are different from those of another member and the other person does not give any indication of respecting or understanding the differing viewpoint.

● ● ● ● ●

Counterproductive Leader Behaviors

Here is a list of some common counterproductive leader behaviors. Many of these are unconscious or unintentional on the part of the leader, but that does not diminish the negative impact they can have on the group and its members:

- Empathic failures that begin with a personal statement used to rationalize lack of attention to members' communications, lack of interest, or as being focused on important/urgent personal concerns.

- A lack of an emotional presence, which signals a lack of emotional investment in a particular group member or in the group overall.

- Overly explaining because of a need to have members like and approve of him or her.

- Inappropriate self-disclosure, one-up-manship, bragging, boasting and behavior intended to bring attention to oneself.

- A lack of empathy where the leader is unable or unwilling to be empathic or respond empathically.

- An unrealistic expectation of self and of others to be perfect.

- Works on personal issues in the group and has group members take care of him or her instead of taking care of the group members.

- Fails to monitor possible countertransference.

- Fails to stay in touch with the impact of his or her actions on group members, such as what can happen during a confrontation.

- Exploits group members for personal, psychological, or emotional gains.

- Misuses charm, charisma.

- Plays favorites among group members.

- Manipulates, coerces, or pushes group members to do what the leader wants.

- Is pleased when group members cry, become distressed, and the like as he or she considers this to be a breakthrough; that is, the leader is more focused on personal reactions than on being empathic with the group member.

- Makes devaluing, minimizing, demeaning remarks, or is overly complimentary;
- Fails to adequately monitor the group's physical and psychological boundaries;
- Personalizes members' comments, remarks, and the like;
- Suppresses, ignores, or otherwise avoids conflict; or instigates conflict.

4

• • • • •

Open Groups:
Challenges and Benefits

Julia was assigned to facilitate a mixed gender group of young adults who were working on relationship issues. This group was advertised as an open group that would meet weekly for 24 weeks. The open group was formed to take into account members' work, school, and family schedules. Julia had planned the group to focus on issues identified by members and the group and to develop their communication skills and relating attributes. All members attended the first two sessions, agreed on the goals for the group, and set personal goals. As the group progressed, Julia found herself becoming frustrated and somewhat disappointed. It seemed that whatever she planned for a session could not be accomplished because of members' absences. For example, it was impossible to follow-up on a member's intense emotional disclosure when the member did not appear at the next session. Or, group members would not explore or discuss the previous session's topic, disclosures, or theme, but focused instead on a new member entering the group. Or, a conflict that emerged in one session could not be discussed or resolved because one, both, or some members were absent in subsequent sessions.

Julia was an experienced group leader but all of her previous groups were closed groups with a defined membership and life span. Although she was cognitively prepared to facilitate an open group, she was not emotionally prepared and the constraints taxed her perceptions of her competence, which in turn led to her feelings of frustration and disappointment. She even made comments in the group about the inability to follow up on important topics that had emerged. The group picked up on her frustration and disappointment on some level, and reacted in a variety of ways that went unrecognized by Julia as possible reactions to her feelings and perceptions of the group. Examples of members' indirect reactions included absenteeism, increasing the number of side conversations and other disruptive activities, withdrawal exhibited by more members becoming and staying silent, and a disinclination to explore issues and topics that emerged in the group. These behaviors only added to Julia's frustration and disappointment.

This scenario is presented to illustrate what can happen when the group leader is not aware of the constraints for an open group, and is not emotionally prepared to address these. Caring and conscientious group leaders work hard to provide a positive and constructive group experience for the group members, and have a desire to facilitate their growth, development, and healing, but the constraints of the open group have to be fully understood in advance. Some of the knowledge and experience of closed groups can be transferred to open groups, but the open group is sufficiently different so that some knowledge and experiences do not fit the new circumstances, and the group leader needs to be aware that some perceptual shifts are needed.

Chapters 4, 5, and 6 address the unique characteristics and needs of open groups. The material applies the basics of group such as planning, leader preparation and facilitation, group stages, the therapeutic alliance, and therapeutic factors to this type of group. Chapter 4 presents the definition, description, benefits, and constraints for open groups. Chapter 5 focuses on a brief description of the significant issues and concerns facing open group leaders, and describes a planning process. Chapter 6 discusses leader preparation and facilitative strategies that can be used, and presents some activities for open groups.

● ● ● ● ●

Definition and Description

Leaders who facilitate open groups understand in advance that attendance will be inconsistent, that members will terminate from the group at different times, and that new members can be added at different times. However, they are unlikely to have been prepared by their training programs on how to deal with many group situations in open groups, especially those that can usually be addressed in groups where attendance is regular or where new members are not added or members terminate before the agreed upon number of sessions are completed.

Open groups were defined in chapter 1 as having the following characteristics:

■ Being organized around a common theme or purpose;

■ The life span or duration of the group may or may not be specified in advance of the group's beginning;

■ New members may be added at any time;

- Members may terminate at any or different points in the life of the group;
- There is usually inconsistent member attendance at group sessions;
- Screening or orientation of members may not be possible;
- Group members may be voluntary or have mandated attendance.

These open groups are found in many settings, such as hospitals, especially for the inpatient population; in agencies; and in some mental health preparation programs, such as T-groups for resident physicians in psychiatry. The most prevalent open groups are self-help and support groups, although some treatment groups are also open ended.

Benefits

It is easier to list the constraints for open groups than it is the benefits. However, it can be helpful to stay aware that there can be some positive aspects to open groups, and leaders can help both themselves and group members by understanding that the constraints can be mediated. Benefits for members include the following:

- Members can experience some of Yalom and Leszcz's (2005) therapeutic factors, such as universality, altruism, and hope that promote healing, growth, and development.
- They are provided with a safe place to openly express distressful feelings.
- They learn new information and how to apply it.
- They receive feedback from others and provide feedback to others.
- They experience positive ways to behave and relate.
- They reduce feelings of isolation, loneliness, and alienation, and provide social support to others.

Experience Therapeutic Factors

The therapeutic factor of universality can more easily emerge in open groups because these groups are usually formed around a common theme or condition. Group members can be guided to understand the commonalties they have that go beyond surface characteristics and experiences, and the issue or condition that brought them to the group (Agazarian, 1997). Deeper connections include having similar reactions and feelings about themselves, events, and their life experiences;

how the issues or conditions affect self-perception and relationships; fears and apprehensions they hold, although these may differ in kind and in intensity; and other such important commonalties. This therapeutic factor can be capitalized on regardless of the constraints of an open group.

Altruism often goes unrecognized but it still has an impact. It is defined as freely giving of oneself without expectations of reward or reciprocity. Recipients for altruistic acts can feel valued and understood, and providers can experience the pleasure that comes from giving to others (Hafen, Karren, Frandsen, & Smith, 1996). There are many kindnesses that members can give to each other, and the leader can model this. Examples of altruistic acts in the group are as follows:

- Verbalizing a recognition of someone's difficulties even when that person does not verbalize these;
- Pointing out a fellow group member's unrecognized strength or a positive aspect of his or her self;
- Complements that are sincere and are heartfelt;
- Words of encouragement and support;
- Providing empathic responses.

It is important that group members experience hope as this will give them a rationale for continuing. Some open groups address significant physical and emotional conditions and issues that have a negative impact on functioning and quality of life. Examples include recovering from a physical illness or condition, adjusting to needed changes as a result of being ill or injured, coping with a chronic state either physical or psychological, and other similar states. It is when the common theme or purpose for the group centers on situations such as those in the examples, that the possibility of achieving realistic hope is a significant benefit.

Realistic hope will be defined as a state that provides courage to cope and adjust successfully, but not a false or unrealistic expectation of causing the adversity or ordeal to disappear. The value of being hopeful cannot be underestimated as it can fuel persistence in the face of obstacles and setbacks, provide determination to have as much quality of life as possible, and support an expectation that one's efforts will be rewarded in some way (Hopper, 2001). Hope keeps the future alive and possible.

These are just three examples of how therapeutic factors can emerge or be fostered in the group. Other therapeutic factors, such as dissemination of information, catharsis, socializing techniques, and existential concerns can also be a part of the open group's factors. Modeling by the group leader is possible, but capitalizing on members' imitative behaviors can be more problematic. Possibly the therapeutic factor that will be the most difficult to achieve is group cohesion because of the inconsistent attendance and changing membership. It is not impossible for the group to become somewhat cohesive, but group cohesion as described by Yalom (1995) can be difficult to develop and will almost certainly take longer than would be expected if the group had a closed structure.

As you can see there are many important benefits that an open group can offer its members. Although it is challenging to have to cope with a dynamic and sometimes unexpected structure, the open group can be a positive source for learning, growing, and healing when the group leader perceives the challenges as unavoidable and works to highlight the benefits these groups can convey.

Feeling Expression

The group can sometimes be the only place where some members can openly express distressing thoughts, feelings, and ideas without fear of offending a loved one, coworker, or friend. More importantly, the expression can be understood, echoed, and has the possibility of being explored and ameliorated to some extent. Distressing feelings are difficult to tolerate, both for self and for others, and so, the individual may suppress or deny distressing feelings. Or, if the feelings are expressed, others can try to minimize or ignore them; some may rationalize them, some members try to talk the person out of having the feelings, and other actions that illustrate an inability to accept the feelings. The group can be a place where expressing such feelings is acceptable and understood, thereby providing relief and validation for the person (Castonguay, Pincus, Agras, & Hines, 1998).

Receive New Information

Almost all open groups have an information dissemination component and this can be an enormous benefit for group members. New information could include the following:

- Strategies to cope with the condition or situation associated with the topic or issue;
- Research findings on progression, causes, or prognosis;
- More effective ways to communicate;
- Stress reduction techniques.

Group members as well as the group leader, and in some instances, an outside expert, can all contribute to providing information.

Receive and Give Feedback

The group can be a place where members learn and practice effective ways to both receive and give feedback because the group is a safer place for these acts to occur when the leader is trained and capable. Some members may have experienced feedback as negative because it was presented in a manner that was wounding to the receiver, or the content was threatening in some way. The group setting can be a place where after safety and trust are established, and genuineness and respect are modeled and encouraged, feedback can be taught and learned. Members can grow in their awareness of their self, and of their impact on others, both of which can be useful in the group and in their relationships outside the group (Brown, 2009).

Positive Ways to Behave and Relate

The group can be a place to learn and practice more positive ways of behaving and relating, ways that would improve relationships. Members can learn the importance of listening, responding to the feelings in a communication and not just the content, the impact of empathy and unrepaired empathic failures, nonverbal indices of warmth and caring, and other related attributes and communication skills (MacKenzie, 1990). The following story illustrates the positive benefits for a member that took place outside the group:

> Lucas had learned about empathic failures in the group class and in the T-group experience connected to the class. He experienced first-hand the impact of empathic failures on himself and on other group members, both giving and receiving these. He also experienced how relationships were positively impacted by repair of empathic failures.
>
> His family gathered for a holiday, and when his father said something to his sister that he felt was insensitive, Lucas immediately told his father that what he said was not empathic. To his father's credit and others who were present when this occurred, they wanted to know what Lucas meant. He explained about empathic responding, empathic failure, and empathic failure repair. After the holiday, Lucas reported to the instructor about the event and the outcome. He told the professor that the rest of the holiday was harmonious and pleasurable as each family member tried to make their communications more empathic. Lucas said that he felt for the first time that no one left with hurt feelings about what someone had said to him or her.

This is a true story with some details changed to maintain anonymity. It illustrates the power and potential for learning new ways to communicate and relate.

Isolation, Loneliness, Alienation, and Social Support

Although the digital age has promoted communication, the existential factors of isolation, loneliness, and alienation still persist. Activities or being in a crowd are not adequate substitutes for meaningful, satisfying, and enduring relationships, and these can be difficult for some to initiate. Thus, people can feel isolated, experience loneliness, and in some ways also feel alienated, as if others are able to connect and form intimate relationships that they cannot or do not.

Not all who feel this way are also physically isolated. Indeed, some may be very active, have a busy social life, and know many people. However, it is the inner connections to others and emotional intimacy that they long for and do not feel that they have. The group provides an opportunity to form new relationships; reduce those feelings of being isolated, lonely, and alienated; and increase connections to others as well as working on the issue, concern, or the like as they participate in group sessions (Leszcz, 2012).

● ● ● ● ●

Constraints

The major constraints of open groups were listed in the definition at the beginning of this chapter. Those will be explored in more detail here, as will the additional constraint that relates to the leader. Perhaps, the most significant constraint can be the preparation and perceptions of the group leader, even group leaders who are experienced with facilitating these groups. By that, I mean that the group leaders' attitudes, how they manage and contain their personal emotions, the extent of their personal growth and development can be either enhancers for the group, or constraints. We'll discuss how these can be constraints along with suggestions for why they are important, and how to moderate or change them.

The constraints in the definition are: an unspecified group life span; adding new members at any time; members can terminate at any time; inconsistent attendance; lack of screening or pregroup orientation; and mandated attendance.

An Unspecified Life Span for the Group

When the group does not have a specified life span, the leader is unable to have members participate in a planned and orderly termination process. Such a process provides all members with an opportunity to learn how to end relationships in a positive and constructive manner; to complete any unfinished business that they may have; to openly speak to others and to the leader about what they have achieved or learned, and to hear others do the same; to reflect on and celebrate any personal changes they have experienced; to be able to allow themselves to get in touch with their feelings of grief and loss and work through these; and to be able to reflect on the positive and negative impact of the group on them, and other such relevant topics. The open group life span can be very helpful for some groups, especially self-help and support groups, but they lack specificity for the duration of the group which can be unsettling for some group members. There are no definitive time boundaries.

The Addition of New Members

One of the defining characteristics for many open groups is that new members can be added at any time. Adding new members to replace those that are leaving can be very helpful, and can keep the group viable. However, it can also be unsettling for some members and for some leaders to not have consistent membership. The new person is not just an additive event; he or she also brings new variables that must be considered, such as a different personality, perspective, condition, relating skills set, interpersonal communications, and the like. The remaining group members will then have to make an adjustment to the new person(s), may be wary and cautions because they do not know the person, become less trusting for the same reason, and the group can literally take one or more steps backwards in its development.

Members Can/Will Terminate from the Group

The open group has an expectation that one or more members will terminate during the group's life span. This termination can occur when the member has reached his or her goals for attending group, when the member and the leader both agree that the group is no longer viable for that person, or when life circumstances change so that group attendance is no longer possible. These situations allow the group leader to plan for termination and to be prepared for the possible impact on the group and on the remaining members. A process for planned termination is discussed in the next chapter.

Inconsistent Attendance

This constraint is discussed in other places in the book because it has a significant impact on what the leader can do as well as having an impact on the group members. Group leaders have to be mentally prepared not to have an opportunity to follow through on topics, issues, and events that occur in a session because the principal participants may not attend the following session where they could be reintroduced to the group and the prior discussion built on. For example, suppose that a group member begins a confrontation or feedback to another group member in a session, but it doesn't feel as if it is resolved or sufficiently explored. The leader cannot plan on doing so in the next session because one or both participants may be absent. This is the kind of situation that can be very frustrating to group leaders because of timing, feelings, and thoughts that are left dangling and unresolved, and a fruitful discussion with other group members is truncated because the major participant(s) are not present.

Screening and Pregroup Orientation

Screening and pregroup orientation are shown to relate to positive outcomes for the group (Brown, 2006; Gans & Alonso, 1998; Yalom & Leszcz, 2005). However, numerous open groups will not screen prospective group members, and few if any self-help or support groups screen to determine member suitability for the group. If there is a group leader, that person will be able to interview or screen group members. Pregroup orientation is also problematic but could be helpful in preparing group members to enter an existing group. This will reduce some of the ambiguity and uncertainty for the new member, can help reduce some of the fear and trepidation they can have, and acquaint them with the expectations for what they can gain, the usual behaviors expected in the group, and other such valuable information. In the absence of these, the group leader will have to work harder to integrate the new member, and to also address the needs of the remaining members.

Mandated Attendance

Many of the constraints for mandated attendance will apply to both open and closed groups. However, there can be significantly more negative impacts with an open group. Extensive resistance, hostility, rigid defensiveness, and the like are usual behaviors and attitudes for group members who are mandated to attend. These members will likely enter the group with resentment, feel powerless, perceive that they have little or no control, can be fearful of being judged in a negative way, and can be vengeful. All of these states will have a negative impact on their performance in the group, and can also have a negative influence on other group members.

● ● ● ● ●

The Group Leader's Attitude

Both entry level and experienced group leaders have and communicate attitudes about the open group and its members although each may be different. The entry level group leaders' attitudes come from expectations, while the experienced leaders' attitudes are formed from experiences they have encountered when leading such groups. Experienced group leaders know better what to expect, and their attitudes can reflect their dismay about the constraints while entry level group leaders can be disoriented by the unexpected challenges that emerge.

Possible attitudes that group leaders can have that can be constraints:

■ Open groups are not effective and can be somewhat futile.

■ Members receive substandard or little help.

■ Cohesion is impossible to develop.

■ At best, this open group experience is a Band-Aid.

Now, none of these are openly verbalized except perhaps to supervisors or other peer group leaders, and some group leaders may not even be aware that they hold these attitudes. However, these attitudes can affect their facilitation of the group, especially on the nonconscious level. When skepticism or lack of faith in the group is communicated in any way to group members, it is possible that they catch those attitudes and feelings and are influenced by them in their perception of the value of the group and the extent of their participation.

The open group's structure can lead to these attitudes because the attendance and other factors can interfere with the development of several positive group dynamics and factors such as learning to give and receive feedback, exploration of personal feelings and past experiences, trust in the group leader and other group members, group cohesion, moderating or reducing resistance, accepting group process commentary, and so on. When an open group continues long enough with relatively stable membership, many of these dynamics and factors can and do develop, but many open groups have a limited life span and unstable group membership.

Instead of dwelling on the unattainable group possibilities, it may be better for the group leader to have faith that the constraints do not prevent some group members from deriving some benefits. Even though the benefits can be modest, any help is better than no help at all, group members can be helpful to each other even if the desired third stage of group development, cohesion, is not accessed. Band-Aids serve a very useful purpose in preventing further injury or infection.

Manage and Contain Personal Emotions

Group leaders can model successful management and containment of personal emotions and thereby teach group members how to do this for themselves. Leaders can experience frustration, deflation or depression, anger, guilt, and other negative feelings about the structure and constraints of the open group, especially if they feel that the structure and constraints make the group less rich and hopeful than would be the case in other types of groups.

Even when a group leader does not speak of his or her negative emotions, these may be conveyed or projected onto the group where some or all members can receive them on top of the distressful emotions members are bringing into the session. Since neither the group leader nor the members may be aware of the projecting and catching, that is, projective identification, there can be nonconscious negative effects on the group and its members. However, it is essential that the group leader not work on his or her feelings and attitudes in the group, but save this work for supervision or personal therapy. The leader's ability to manage and contain personal emotions is critical for the group's functioning and serves as a model for group members.

Level of Personal Development

The level of the group leader's personal development also plays a significant role in his or her perceptions of the group, the relationships established with other group members, feelings experienced, and in knowing how and when to intervene. Why then can this be a constraint?" The level of the leader's personal development can act as a constraint for an open group when the leader does the following:

- Becomes frustrated about inconsistent attendance;
- Blames group members for resistance;
- Is unable to recognize members' transference, resistance, or projections;
- Fails to recognize empathic failures and work to repair these in the sessions;
- Expects members to buy into and follow his or her agenda exclusively;
- Has an attitude that he or she knows what is best for members and allows no or few deviations;

- Works harder on content than process;
- Incorporates a defeatist or futile attitude into the work, feeling that the structure is not good enough for real work to be accomplished.

A good or acceptable level of personal development on the other hand, enriches the group experience in the following ways:

- Permits acceptance of the group's structure and finds creative ways to enrich and enhance this;
- Focuses more on what can than what cannot be done;
- Accepts members where they are at this point and recognizes that they are doing the best that they can;
- Responds empathically without inferences about should or ought;
- Recognizes and accepts that resistance is used to protect the person and leaves it alone;
- Values the therapeutic alliance and works to establish this with every member;
- Understands that the establishment of trust and safety is fundamental to the group, that it can be difficult or impossible for some members because of their life experiences, and has a realistic expectation for the degree of trust and safety that can be developed;
- Be less self-absorbed and focus more on group members and their needs;
- Stay aware of countertransference, and learn to use it in a constructive way;
- These are some of the positive and constructive ways that the leader's level of personal development can be helpful to the group and its members, rather than being a constraint.

The next chapter presents six significant issues and concerns for open groups, and suggests possible strategies to address these.

5

• • • • •

Open Groups:
Issues, Concerns, and
Possible Strategies

Five significant issues confront leaders of an open group: voluntary versus involuntary group members; inconsistent attendance; screening and orientation; integrating new members; and planned or premature termination. Some of these issues and concerns also apply to other types of groups, but can be more influential on open groups as they are closely related to establishing trust and safety, the therapeutic alliance; addressing group level concerns such as group level resistance; the emergence of therapeutic factors; moving through or developing group stages; and other group functions and factors. This discussion will focus on describing the six significant issues and concerns listed as they relate to the open group, and suggestions are provided for how to address these. Also addressed are the importance for planning and a suggested planning procedure.

• • • • •

Voluntary versus Involuntary Members

Open groups, such as self-help and support groups, usually have voluntary group members who exhibit many of the behaviors and attitudes of constructive group members, such as commitment to the group, willingness to disclose and participate, and motivation to attend sessions (Yalom & Leszcz, 2005). These are the member factors that enhance the group as well as promoting growth, development, and healing for the group members. Even when the constraints of open groups are present, these member characteristics contribute in positive ways to the group's functioning and progress.

However, there are some open groups that have involuntary members; that is, these members are forced to attend, which presents some constraints and barriers in time-bound groups, and these are intensi-fied in open groups. Constraints and barriers for involuntary members are usually their perceptions and feelings about having to do something they do not want to do, skepticism about the positive benefits or out-comes for them personally, resentment about their involuntary atten-dance, and a feeling of helplessness. These are difficult for the group leader to manage under the best of conditions, and the characteristics and structure of an open group just add to the difficulties. The group leader has to cope with and manage the usual group factors, but now also has to find ways to manage the additional negative behaviors and attitudes for these members. The group leader should expect that the development of safety and trust will be delayed or even impossible to establish to a level where members engage in significant disclosures; resistance may be intense and continue for the duration of the group; there can be attempts to undermine the leader's authority; some mem-bers may openly refuse to participate; members may work hard to keep the group at a trite or surface level; and some defensive and negative feelings will get displaced on the leader. A leader has to have a high level of preparation, self-development, and self-confidence to facilitate an open group of involuntary members.

● ● ● ● ●

Inconsistent Attendance

In addition to other concerns, there can be inconsistent attendance due to resistance, unexpected life events, illnesses, and so on. There should be an agreed on rule about attendance from the very beginning of the group because the group can be severely affected when members miss sessions. Even though most absences may be inadvertent and under-standable, attendance is one way of gauging commitment to the group, the importance or lack of importance of the group for the missing mem-bers, and the additional constraints this presents to developing trust and safety, the therapeutic alliance, and group cohesion. Leaders may want to consider having a specific number of sessions that can be missed, making it clear to group members that missing more than that number can result in termination from the group or referral to other modes of treatment. Some absences can be excused, and sensitivity shown for absences out of the control of the member, such as an extended illness. Consistent members' attendance for the group, even when attendance is involuntary:

■ Reduces uncertainty;

■ Provides opportunities for making meaningful connections;

■ Promotes universality;

■ Supports a positive group climate;

■ Models a sense of responsibility and commitment.

Groups, by their very nature, can be anxiety producing for members because of their ambiguity and uncertainty. Members, even experienced group members, can feel anxious in new situations, not knowing what to expect or being unsure as to what is expected of them. The very nature of open groups that do not have certain boundaries or defining points, such as beginnings, endings, and a consistent membership, means that the anxiety about ambiguity and uncertainty can continue longer that it does for other groups, although these may be reduced as the group continues. However, this anxiety about ambiguity and uncertainty can be easily aroused when group members do not know who will be attending from session to session because of inconsistent attendance, the introduction of new members, and the termination of members, all of which leads to the group leader having to continually cope with this basic anxiety. This anxiety can prevent the group from coalescing and providing sufficient trust and safety so that members can begin to grow, develop, and heal.

One of the benefits for participating in a group is the opportunity to make meaningful connections. Members who are inconsistent with their attendance can find that this opportunity for meaningful connections is reduced because other members can be wary of extending themselves for fear of abandonment as manifested by the uncertainty about that member's attendance. Hence, members can be even more tentative about making connections and the group's climate can suffer as a result.

Universality is a very important group dynamic and it is recommended that it be fostered from the beginning of the group because it contributes to the building of feelings of trust and safety, of members feeling accepted and valued, and as the group progresses, can provide hope by seeing others improve or develop coping strategies. So, when attendance is inconsistent, universality can be reduced or impaired.

Promoting the therapeutic alliance fosters positive group and member progress, and it becomes more difficult to establish this alliance with individual members who make up the group when there is inconsistent attendance. The group's climate is produced by the quality of the therapeutic relationship that is established, members' feelings about each other and the leader, and the group experience. To be positive requires the leader's ability to establish a warm, receptive, and accepting relationship with each group member and this can be affected by the member's attendance. The climate is already influenced and impacted by the characteristics of an open group, so that inconsistent attendance becomes more of an issue than it would in other types of groups.

Members who consistently attend group sessions are modeling responsibility and commitment. They have made an explicit or implicit contract and they are honoring the contract. This is a positive behavior that is nonconsciously conveyed to others and can be one of the therapeutic factors: imitative behavior. Other group members can pick up on the behavior and seek to imitate it when the group leader notices and reinforces it in a way that is encouraging.

A strategy to address inconsistent behavior would have the leader acknowledge members' absences and have present members comment on how the absence affects them and the group. And, when the absent member returns, acknowledge his or her presence and how the group is different in a positive way because the former absentee has rejoined the group. Another strategy is to acknowledge members who are present and their contributions to the group.

● ● ● ● ●

Screening and Orientation

The group leader may not be in a position where screening for group suitability can be done, such as when members are mandated to attend the group. In addition, some open groups have a practice of accepting anyone who is interested in the group. Screening is a valuable process that can prevent some problems for the group and for the potential group member (Gans & Alonso, 1998).

It is helpful to have a screening process and group leaders are encouraged to use one whenever possible, especially when someone wants to join an already existing group as is usually the case with open groups. This can be a process to use even when the leader cannot refuse admission to the group, e.g. members are mandated to attend.

An Example of the Screening Process

1. Obtain background data such as a social history.
2. Set up an interview prior to the proposed date of entry to the group.
3. Develop a set of questions prior to the interview such as the following:

   ■ Tell me what you think the group will be like, such as what do you think is required of you as a group member.

   ■ What do you think is the purpose of the group and how do you perceive your needs will be met in this group?

   ■ Do you have any personal goals you want to achieve?

- What will be your contributions to the group (attendance, responding to others, and the like)?
- Do you have any apprehensions or reservations about joining the group?

Even when screening is not an option, group leaders will find it helpful to have an orientation to the group session, and this is highly recommended for new members entering an existing group. In this instance, both the new and existing group members need some orientation. Such sessions help to reduce some of the ambiguity and uncertainty for both. Bringing a new member into a group is not a simple addition; it brings a complication that changes everything from the group climate to inter-member relationships. Orientation can help ease this transition (refer to chapter 1 for suggested orientation topics).

● ● ● ● ● ●

Integrating New Members

It can be helpful for the group leader to be flexible when integrating a new member into the group because existing group members may behave in unexpected ways, and he or she should expect that this integration is a process that can last for several sessions. This process begins two or more sessions prior to the event, with the leader informing members that a new member will be joining the group. The leader should allow members to discuss the impact of this event and other thoughts and feelings, and then he or she should present a structure for the meeting with the new member involved, and invite them to present their ideas for a smooth transition. At the same time, however, refrain from providing too much information about the new member, limiting this to the basics such as gender, and an acknowledgment of the common problem or concern facing the group if this is appropriate. The new member should decide on how much personal information is to be shared with the group both prior to and upon joining the group.

There are some conditions and situations to avoid for the initial session: a barrage of questions directed at the new member or intrusive questions; letting the new member engage in extended storytelling; ignoring the new member; allowing the new person to become the "identified patient"; hostile or aggressive remarks and comments directed to the person or by that person; or a focus on his or her differences from other group members. It is important to remember that the pattern for inclusion/exclusion will be set at the first session and negative effects once established will be difficult to overcome.

Positive integration strategies include the following:

- Facilitating introductions by directing the new and existing members about what to disclose as an introduction; such as occupation, goal(s) for group participation, what the person hopes to gain from participation, or a piece of personal information they are comfortable disclosing.
- Ensure that both new and existing members are introduced.
- Focus on feelings experienced in the introductions.
- Link and emphasize similarities among the new and existing members, but only the similarities openly disclosed in the introduction. Do not use information revealed in previous sessions or from the screening/ orientation.
- If some group members are absent at the session where the new member enters the group, acknowledge this absence and be prepared for additional introductions when they return.

● ● ● ● ●

Planned Termination

All groups have members who terminate the group, either individually or collectively, such as when a group ends. Since open groups may not have a definitive ending date or time, a collective termination is unlikely to occur. Leaders of open groups encounter individual members who terminate, either planned or on a premature basis that is unplanned and unanticipated. Planned terminations provide space and time for the group member, group leader, and other group members to prepare for closure. Unplanned and premature termination does not leave any time to prepare, which can be frustrating for members and the leader, and trigger feelings and reactions from similar past experiences and family of origin issues. As a result, many unresolved issues and questions may never be answered.

   Planned termination would have a process similar to that of integrating new members: notification in advance; a structure for that member's last session; involving all group members who are present; and being prepared to address residual feelings such as loss or relief.

Example of Planned Termination

It can be helpful to provide group members with a specific date for the terminating member's last session, and to have a planned process for implementation at the last session. The process can include helping the member who is leaving and the remaining group members to say good-bye in a way that reduces or eliminates any unfinished business with that person.

The process can include expressing sadness about the loss of the relationship, verbalizing an appreciation for what the person brought to the group and what the group provided to that person, and hopes and wishes for the future. The session could also bring some measure of resolution overall, or resolution for a specific conflict, and can be an opportunity to repair empathic failures. The entire session could be focused on termination of the relationship, which could also teach group members satisfactory ways to say goodbye; or the departure of the member could be a part of the session. In either case, the situation can provide for some important work to be done.

Whatever the leader decides to do for termination, the most important objective for the session is to ensure that there is sufficient time and space to express members' thoughts and feelings about the termination.

Unplanned termination, such as premature termination, or when life circumstances cause an abrupt termination from the group can be very disruptive and distressing for the leader and for the group. Members can reexperience feelings from their past where relationships were abruptly terminated, which can trigger abandonment issues, fear, and other negative and intense feelings, and the group leader has to be emotionally prepared to deal with these effects whether or not they are directly expressed (also see chapter 10 for managing premature termination).

Template for an Unplanned or Premature Termination

The group leader can use the following procedures to facilitate the unplanned or premature termination of a group member:

1. *Announce the termination to the group. (This assumes that the leader knows in advance of the session that the member intends or needs to terminate.)*
2. *Openly acknowledge its unexpectedness.*
3. *If there is an unavoidable reason for the leaving, such as an illness or unexpected relocation, tell group members the reason. If the reason is a choice, invite the member to tell the group of his or her need to terminate. If the member terminated without notification, discuss what happened with the group, and be careful not to blame that group member.*
4. *Invite group member responses with an emphasis on their feelings.*

5. *Conduct a short reflection on that member's contributions to the group and ask members to speak of these in the session.*
6. *Ask members to verbalize how they think the group may be different without that member.*
7. *Ask if there are any goodbye thoughts or feelings they want to express, or would have expressed if the person was present.*
8. *Invite the terminating member to verbalize his or her feelings about the group, members, and termination.*

The group leader should be prepared to help members express and work through anger, grief, and loss, old feelings around fear of abandonment, indifference, or even relief depending on the relationship with the leaving member.

Planned termination would use many of the same steps, but the sequence and timing may be different because the termination is not an unanticipated or unexpected event. Group leaders should have a rule that they be notified a certain amount of time in advance when a member anticipates leaving the group. It is suggested that notification occurs two or three sessions prior to the termination. The leader or the member can announce the termination and the date for it to the group two or three sessions in advance. After the announcement, the following procedure could be used.

Planned Termination

1. As part of the announcement, the leader tells the group that time will be provided at the last session to say goodbye, and the available group time that remains could be used for the member who is leaving, and for other group members, to finish any unfinished business. The group leader has to take care that goodbyes are not given prematurely by noting how much time is left before the ending.
2. Invite the terminating member and other group members to verbalize and explore their feelings and thoughts.
3. It could be helpful to explore what the member and the group wants to do to say goodbye. It is important that the focus be kept on the group and not be diffused with a social event. Social events can be held after the session.
4. The last session for the terminating member should have the following basic elements: The group notes the member's contributions, and the terminating member expresses what he or she has received from the group and any appreciations the member may wish to express for the group and the leader. Other possibilities are the member's wishes for the future, expressions from the group of support and hopes for gifts such as resilience for the terminating member or greater self-appreciation, and so on.

• • • • •

Planning Open Groups

Although it is challenging, open groups can be planned. The previous two chapters have presented the benefits, constraints, and significant issues and concerns that need to be considered when planning and facilitating the open group. Planning involves setting goals and objectives, developing guidelines and rules, designing activities, and assessment. Prior to the start of the formal planning, the group leader should perform the following preplanning tasks:

■ Describe the type of group;

■ Identify the target audience;

■ Determine the probable member characteristics and abilities;

■ Decide on the purpose for the group;

■ Read research outcomes from the professional literature.

• • • • •

Type of Group

Several types of groups can be conducted as open groups, such as the following:

■ Educational groups may focus on acquiring a specific body of knowledge; for example, a group for parent education.

■ Psychoeducational groups are very often time-limited closed groups, but some can be open groups. These groups will have a balance of cognitive and affective functions where knowledge acquisition is as important as a focus on feelings.

■ Support and self-help groups are designed to provide information, hope, and encouragement around a commonly held members' issue or condition.

■ Long-term psychotherapy groups will have members added or terminated, and some members of such groups may drop out for a period of time but do return.

Many open groups have an educational component and this can be difficult to manage because there are new members entering at different points and with different understandings about the common topic. Existing members have information the new members do not have, and can get turned off or bored at the repetitiveness involved in bringing the new members up to speed. Leaders must remain mindful of both sets of needs and plan to accommodate both.

Target Audience

There are several ways to conceptualize the target audience but the most important categories are age and volunteer/mandated status. Planning will be different for the various age groups and the leader needs to use the age group as a guide. Is the group intended for children (e.g., 6–12), adolescents (e.g., 13–19), young adults (e.g., 20–40), late adults (e.g., 41–60), or seniors (e.g., 61+)? While a mixture of ages may not be relevant to the topic, the age range for the group can play a role in what and how information will be disseminated, member to member interactions, and for members' willingness to participate. Further, it can be inadvisable to have very young group members in groups with older members, and for some groups, the gender and age of group members can make a difference. This can be especially important since prohibition of out of group contact and socializing may not be enforceable.

Member Characteristics

Many or most open groups are organized around a common theme or issue, so some member characteristics can be known in advance, which assists with planning. Characteristics such as probable age, gender, educational level, diagnosis, and prognosis can be anticipated. This information allows the group leader to decide on modes or methods of presentation, the reading level for materials, primary concerns that need to be addressed around the group's common issue or condition, and other concerns that are likely to emerge. Goals, objectives, and strategies can be selected to better fit the group's purpose and members' needs.

Purpose

Group leaders can find it challenging to clearly define the purpose for the group because of important competing member needs. For example, a support group can have important needs for disseminating information, providing opportunities for emotional expression, developing relationships and social support, teaching coping skills, and so on. It is tempting to try and make all of these the focus of the group, but the reality is that, while all have a role and may be addressed in some form, if all are the purposes for the group it will become diffused and no one need or topic will be adequately addressed. Having a clear purpose provides focus, direction, and structure for what is presented and for meeting members' needs.

Literature

It is important to conduct a review of the professional literature when planning a group. Many open groups are organized to address a common issue or concern and there is some information to be disseminated, so reviewing the research findings about these groups and their members can be helpful for planning. It is recommended that a review of the literature be conducted even when the leader is knowledgeable because new understandings and information are constantly emerging that could be helpful to group members. While a review of the professional literature is recommended, a review of material about the issue or concern written for the lay public could also be helpful. Group members may request referrals to resources they can read on their own, or the group leader may find a resource that could be helpful in their presentations. Some books and articles written for the general public have valuable material.

● ● ● ● ●

Planning Tasks

After the preplanning tasks are completed, the group leader can plan for the open group sessions. It is recommended that the planning be set out in a document that can serve as a guide and structure for the sessions. It could come in handy if a substitute group leader is needed, an eventuality that should be considered at the planning stage. The document can be an outline or a detailed plan. Composing a document helps organize the material to provide for sequencing and may suggest modes for presentations and other strategies. Given the ambiguity and uncertainty that is characteristic of open groups, the plan can help reduce some of this for the group leader, and by extension, for the group members. The planning document should address the following topics: goal(s) and objectives, strategies used to attain these, and assessment of outcomes.

Goals and Objectives

These are the guiding principles for the group that are derived from the purpose. Goals should be limited to one or two major goals that are capable of being assessed. Too many goals lead to confusion and diffusion where the group does not have a clear direction, and can get sidetracked into unproductive actions. Where are you going, how will you get there, and how will you know that you have arrived are the three most important questions, and developing a goal is the first step.

It can be tempting to try and have goals to meet the many different needs that group members can have, but it is also impossible or unlikely that this particular group will be able to meet all or most needs for each group member. Recognizing and accepting the limitations of what can be reasonably done with the group provides clearer directions and reduces frustration. Group leaders care about and are concerned for their group members, but that doesn't mean they should try to "fix" everything because that attitude dilutes the effectiveness of what will be done.

Following is a process for developing the goal for your open group:

> *Sit in silence with no distractions and allow an image to emerge of who your group members are likely to be. This image includes what you know about the common issue or concern; the likely demographic characteristics of group members such as age and gender; what you gleamed from the literature about the group's needs for information, encouragement, and support; relationship issues that could emerge; and so on. Take time to reflect on all of these aspects.*
>
> *Next, reflect on the basic structure and nature of the open group you will lead and give particular attention to the barriers and constraints. For example, it may not be possible to have sequential dissemination of information where material presented assumes or builds on material presented earlier as all group members may not have the previous knowledge. The open group characteristics are the overlay for the group's characteristics and needs.*
>
> *Try to bring all of these reflective thoughts together and add your feelings about what constitutes success. Your feelings will be an important component as you formulate the goals for the group because you too have to end up with a feeling of success and accomplishment. When you feel ready, write one or two major goals for the group.*

Objectives are the steps you will take to reach the goal. For example, if the goal is to build feelings of self-competency for group members, the objectives will be the points along the way to try and accomplish that goal. These objectives might include the following:

- Determine the base level for members' current feelings of self-competency.
- Identify external barriers and constraints that affect self-competency and test their validity.
- Identify internal barriers and constraints and test their validity.

- Identify and highlight inner strengths and resources that can facilitate the growth of feeling competent.
- Create self-affirmations to emphasize strengths.
- Teach strategies to use when members encounter barriers, constraints, and adversity.

These objectives now suggest techniques and strategies and, although it may be best if these are used sequentially to build on each other, they could also be viewed as separate for the open group where members may have inconsistent attendance. Missing a session would not mean that they did not have sufficient information to profit from the next session they attend.

The next step is to identify which strategies you intend to use. Your training and theoretical perspective will play major roles in your choice of strategies. For example, strategies for the sample list of objectives could include teaching distracting techniques and thought-stopping, imagery, communication skills, and conflict resolution. All of these can be beneficial to members, but each could be used separately. It could also be helpful for members to practice some of them outside the group and report the outcomes to the group.

The final planning step is to decide on how you will assess the outcomes. Your assessment should be built in at the beginning so as to make provisions for members who terminate along the course of the group as well as those who stay to the end. The assessment can provide valuable information for the group leader as to what was effective and what was not: Was there growth and development for members, what learning occurred, what is or was needed, especially if this was not anticipated in the initial planning, and what progress was made in accomplishing the goals?

There are assessment techniques and instruments that would be helpful and readers are encouraged to seek these out because it is impossible to provide adequate coverage here. Readers are encouraged to select and use assessment to help with their future group planning or make adjustments for the current group, to assess their efficacy as a group leader, and as part of program evaluation. The last reason could be especially important for funding purposes, such as grants and insurance.

The few techniques and instruments briefly described here are pre- and postsurveys and tests, self-report Likert scales, the semantic differential, and commercial instruments. Readers are encouraged to seek out other techniques and instruments, and to consult with assessment experts.

Pre- and postsurveys and tests provide information related to changes that may occur, perceptions about treatment elements, and other such information. These are administered at the beginning and at or near the end of the group. Developing a survey instrument takes considerable thought, time, and effort, and readers are urged to consult research material on how to construct valid surveys or tests. Tests would be used to determine gains in knowledge and information and this could be important in determining or adjusting the dissemination of information.

A valuable source of information will be the thoughts and feelings of participants about their experiences and their progress. A Likert scale form can be used to gather this information. This scale lists items and asks respondents to choose the number on the scale that best describes their reaction or feeling about the item. The scale usually goes from 1 to 5: for example, 5—extremely worthwhile; 4—very worthwhile; 3—adequate; 2—somewhat worthwhile; 1—not worthwhile. The scale could be applied to items such as the following.

I feel I gained a lot from my group experiences.	5 4 3 2 1
The information provided will be helpful to me.	5 4 3 2 1

The semantic differential is a valid and reliable assessment of attitudes and perceptions, and is easily scored either by obtaining a mean for the checked numbers for the concept being assessed or by using a total score. It also has the advantage of being completed quickly by responders. First decide on what concepts or program components you want to assess. For ease of illustration, let's assume that the group had both an educational and an affective component. The educational component could be assessed on the concepts; the quality of information, usefulness, and the various delivery modes such as lecture, discussion, media, readings, and so on. The affective component could be assessed on the components; helpfulness of group sessions, the leader, and perceived personal growth and development. An example for one item from each component will be illustrated. The next step is to create the semantic differential format of bipolar adjectives to assess the attitudes toward the concept—each concept is presented separately. It is recommended that the same set of adjectives be used for each concept that is assessed so that an overall score for all of the concepts can be derived and compared. The illustration will use the concepts of quality of information and group sessions.

Directions: Check the number between pairs of adjectives that best fit your perception. Example:

Books

Good	9	8	7	6	5	4	3	2	1	Bad
Uninformative	1	2	3	4	5	6	7	8	9	Informative

Information

Good	9	8	7	6	5	4	3	2	1	Bad
Meaningful	9	8	7	6	5	4	3	2	1	Meaningless
Poor	1	2	3	4	5	6	7	8	9	Rich
Dull	1	2	3	4	5	6	7	8	9	Interesting
Helpful	9	8	7	6	5	4	3	2	1	Unhelpful
Boring	1	2	3	4	5	6	7	8	9	Exciting
Applicable	9	8	7	6	5	4	3	2	1	Not applicable

Group Sessions

Not applicable	1	2	3	4	5	6	7	8	9	Applicable
Dull	1	2	3	4	5	6	7	8	9	Exciting
Rich	9	8	7	6	5	4	3	2	1	Poor
Interesting	9	8	7	6	5	4	3	2	1	Dull
Meaningless	1	2	3	4	5	6	7	8	9	Meaningful
Good	9	8	7	6	5	4	3	2	1	Bad
Helpful	9	8	7	6	5	4	3	2	1	Unhelpful

6

• • • • •

Open Groups: Facilitative Skills and Techniques

Chapter 3 addressed basic characteristics and skills that are help-ful for leaders of all types of groups. This chapter focuses on skills and techniques that can be facilitative for open groups with their unique qualities. Seven skills and techniques are presented, each with a ratio-nale for its usefulness and importance, and some have an illustrative activity. Many of these are related to leaders' emotional and psycho-logical states and the extent of their personal growth and development, which are not skills or techniques that can be taught. Skills and tech-niques covered are:

■ Acceptance that group members are doing the best they can at this time;

■ Patience with members' rate of progress;

■ Recognition of incremental improvements;

■ Teach and model positive communication skills;

■ Teach and model positive relating behaviors;

■ Promote the emergence of therapeutic factors;

■ Manage members' difficult behaviors.

• • • • •

Acceptance

Accept that each group member is doing the best that he or she can do at this time and given the circumstances. The member may not be doing very well, but that is where the member is; and acceptance and acknowl-edgment of that central issue can be very empathic and affirming for

the group member. It has the possibility of being encouraging and supportive which can give some members the courage to continue and to
try harder.

The group leader and others in the group members' world want them
to return to being as functional as they were, or to improve and grow and
develop in positive ways. You can also see ways that they could be more
effective, cope better, and the like. There could also be a lot of "if only
he or she would" floating through your mind and through the minds of
group members, as you perceive that things could be better. Any or all
of you may be correct, but this is not helpful because what it conveys is a
lack of understanding of the person both in personal terms and regarding their overall situation at the time, which delays the establishment
of trust. Unless there are homicidal or suicidal behaviors or actions that
are possibly destructive to the safety of that person or others, try to just
accept that the member cannot do better at this time and try to give the
member hope that he or she can and will do better in the future.

Rather than being a set of suggestions of what to do, this skill of
acceptance is focused on what not to do. Try to avoid the following and
block group members from these actions:

1. Asking questions or asking for more detail because you feel that doing
   so indicates interest. It is much more helpful to be willing to accept
   what the person wants to disclose rather than asking questions that
   could seem to the individual in question like an attack.
2. Giving advice to try and be helpful or to "fix" what is perceived as
   being wrong or ineffective for that person.
3. Using disguised ways of telling the person what he or she should or
   ought to do or feel, such as saying what you have done or would do in a
   similar situation. No two situations are the same, and what worked for
   one person may not or will not work for another person.

Acceptance is the deep belief that the group member is doing his or
her best at this time.

Besides not engaging in certain activities, there are some positive
actions that can help to convey acceptance: your emotional presence,
empathic responding, and affirming comments. The group leader
who maintains an emotional presence with the presenting or disclosing member not only conveys that the leader perceives the member as
worthwhile and valued, this emotional presence also allows the leader
to become more empathically attuned to that member, which, in turn,
promotes the ability to give an empathic response (Gans & Alonso, 1998).
Nothing is more effective than an empathic response, which conveys
clearly that the sender has entered the world of the other and is feeling

what that person is feeling. Think about it. You feel accepted by others when you perceive that the other person understands what you mean or are trying to convey. Empathic responses and affirming comments must be spoken aloud even when your nonverbal behavior may be conveying these. Spoken responses can make it clearer to the receiver that you are empathic and affirming. Speaking may be especially helpful when the group members are experiencing emotional intensity because they are more focused on their personal experiencing at this point and less likely to be paying sufficient attention to others to be able to read nonverbal behavior.

Affirming comments are those that convey that you respect, accept, and have positive regard for that person; can also provide hope, support, and encouragement; that you have faith and confidence in the person's ability to cope, grow, and develop; and can identify some strengths or other inner resources they may have that could be helpful for the person.

● ● ● ● ●

Patience

Patience is also needed because group leaders want to see the members' progress in the desired direction, judge their own personal effectiveness by the extent to which members' progress can be seen, and may perceive resistance as willful and arbitrary. Progress is important and to be desired, but group members have to progress at their own rates, not to meet the leader's need.

Components of patience include a clear understanding of oneself as different from others (i.e., boundaries: where you end and where others begin), awareness of countertransference and how this plays a role in your expectations of and for others, and an appreciation for an unfolding process. It sounds so simple to say that others are not you, but it isn't simple to put this understanding into practice. Group members cannot and will not do what you think they should or ought to do, or take actions that you know are helpful or effective, or even act in their own best interests sometimes, and this can be frustrating for the group leader. When this happens, the leader's frustration can be conveyed to the group in conscious and unconscious ways that are likely to produce members' shame, guilt, anger, defiance, and so on. None of these leader-triggered feelings is helpful. Leaders will find it much more constructive to be able to accept that group members will be more willing to take risks, engage in scary self-exploration, reveal hidden material, and present other such productive actions when they feel safe, accepted, and trusting.

● ● ● ● ●

Recognize Incremental Improvements

Encouragement and support are very facilitative and leaders can provide these by openly recognizing members' progress, even incremental progress. Progress can be slow at times, and may not be evident to that person or to others. Helping members focus on their progress can be very rewarding and reinforcing for the particular person, and can provide hope and inspiration for other group members (Yalom & Leszcz, 2005).

Cognitive therapy (Beck, 2000), cognitive behavioral therapy (CBT; Meichenbaum, 1977), dialectical behavior therapy (DBT; Linehan, 1993) and other therapeutic approaches make use of diaries and journals as one way to help show progress as well as highlighting when self-defeating thoughts, feelings, and ideas appear and become triggers for actions. This strategy could be used by group members to build personal awareness, and a variation could be used by the group leader to recognize members' progress, such as group notes that record the leader's observations over time for each member, and when reviewed could provide information that points out subtle or incremental progress.

Journaling

Journaling activity is a useful behavioral technique that can begin when the member enters the group or at the pregroup orientation. This activity asks members to write one or two personal goals when they enter the group, specify the steps needed to achieve the goal(s), and describe indicators of success; that is, how the member will know that the goals have been achieved. Each week members are asked to write a sentence or more about activities or actions they take relative to the goals. This writing can be done outside of the group, or as part of the group session time. They could record thoughts, feelings, barriers or constraints, actions, and outcomes for those actions, and so on. Members could also be encouraged to report on these in the group where it could be easier for others to see visible progress. If this journaling or writing strategy is used, the leader must guide the members in formulating realistic goals that hold some promise of being achieved.

Another positive outcome for the journal writing or a similar strategy, is that the leader then knows the members' goals and their perception of success, which can then be used to monitor incremental progress. It is also possible that the leader can see progress that the member may overlook or ignore.

● ● ● ● ●

Communication Skills

Facilitative techniques include teaching and modeling positive communication skills, such as making verbal communication direct and concrete, listening for content and feelings. Chapters 11 to 13 include activities to teach these communication skills. This discussion will focus on presenting a rationale for why it could be important and helpful for the leader to model and teach these skills.

Every group has an interpersonal aspect and communication skills are important for this aspect as well as being important and critical for the therapeutic factor of teaching socializing skills (Yalom & Leszcz, 2005). The group can be a safe place for members to become aware of deficiencies and to practice new behaviors.

The leader demonstrates through personal example that direct and concrete verbal communication reduces misunderstandings, corrects or clarifies what seems to be misinformation, and promotes authenticity. It is important that the leader not ask rhetorical questions as a way to guide members to where the leader thinks they should go, or to phrase statements as questions; or give statements, responses, comments, and the like that call for them to make inferences about the meaning and intent of the communication, or to be otherwise obscure. Asking questions only for clarification and reducing questioning as probes for more information or as a sign of interest can be helpful in direct and concrete communications.

A basis for empathic responding includes listening for the content and feelings in verbal expressions because the feelings, openly expressed or not, carry the most important part of the message. Communications and relationships are improved when both are heard and responded to. The group leader can demonstrate its efficacy by modeling this in the group, and by emphasizing the importance of being attuned and attentive to the speaker. These are nonverbal behaviors that enhance the ability to listen, such as orienting your body to the speaker, looking at him or her, and maintaining eye contact when appropriate, and the inner state of screening out distractions and thinking about a response. It can be helpful to focus on the speaker and to try and understand the spoken or unspoken feelings.

Empathic responding can be very therapeutic; it strengthens relationships, conveys understanding, respect, and caring, and can help others feel valued. There is a subtle but important difference between being empathic and responding empathically, but that difference is important. Being empathic includes feeling what the other person is feeling without becoming lost, enmeshed in, or overwhelmed by the other person's feelings; you retain the sense of yourself as separate and distinct from the other person. An empathic response on the other hand can mean that you tune in to what the other person is feeling without experiencing those emotions yourself. For example, you can understand that the other person is angry without feeling anger yourself. This is an example of cognitive empathic responding, which is also helpful for relationships such as those with group members, and teaching this to members can enhance the relationships they have with others in their worlds outside of the group.

Constructive confrontation and conflict resolution are also helpful communication skills to teach and model. It is not unusual for group members to have negative perceptions of these and to fear their emergence. Many people can share this perception and reaction because of a family of origin experience and other past relationships. However, neither of these has to be destructive, they can strengthen relationships, and modeling these in the group provides a measure of safety so that members can observe and learn with reduced fears of destruction.

● ● ● ● ●

Relating Skills

The group leader can also teach and model positive relating skills. Members will tend to learn more from what the leader does to establish the therapeutic alliance than they will from a direct effort to teach these skills. Modeling relationship building skills begins at the moment when the leader and members meet each other. That meeting could be at the pregroup interview/screening, or at the first group session. It is important to remember that first impressions count and tend to be lasting, and what is done or said at the initial encounter can set the pattern and tone for the relationship.

Let's define positive relating skills to be the actions that convey to the other person your care for him or her, your concern, respect, and appreciation of the individual's uniqueness and separateness from you and from others, and your interest in establishing a cordial relationship. Many of these skills are your overall nonverbal behaviors. Your face can be the first thing members notice and it carries a powerful message for them. They can consciously or unconsciously notice and react to the extent and duration of your eye contact, whether you orient your body to the speakers, your smiles, and so on. These are clues to the receiver about your feelings and perceptions; for example, frowns convey a different message from smiles. Other nonverbal clues are the sitting position you assume; whether it is open or closed; whether you lean forward slightly to show interest; whether your arms and legs have a relaxed position or not, and the tone of your voice. There are other nonverbal behaviors that also convey messages and readers are encouraged to learn more about them.

Other relating skills that can be taught and modeled by the leader are trustworthiness, which can be conveyed by keeping promises such as confidentiality; genuineness which can be shown in how you are consistent in your treatment of others; and the congruence between your verbal and nonverbal behavior, and the gestures you use to convey a deep understanding of what the other person may be experiencing. It could be helpful to also hold a group discussion on relationship building to get members more aware of how they can initiate and maintain more satisfactory and enduring relationships both inside and outside of the group.

● ● ● ● ●

Therapeutic Factors

The group leader needs to plan to encourage the emergence of group therapeutic factors (Yalom & Leszcz, 2005), especially universality, altruism, hope, and some existential factors such as meaning and purpose. Other therapeutic factors can also be encouraged but are more likely to emerge on their own or to be a focus for the group such as dissemination of information, catharsis, socializing techniques, and interpersonal learning.

Universality around a common issue or concern can be relatively easy to establish when the issue or concern is the focus or purpose for the group, but is more therapeutic when other commonalties are found among group members. Commonalties that can forge deeper and more meaningful connections are those that define the person's identity, values, wishes, hopes, and desires that are growth promoting and positive. While visible similarities can be important for some people, it is the less visible similarities that seem to appeal and draw people together. The group leader can help with this deeper recognition of commonalties through awareness of when these appear in the sessions, and linking them so as to make them apparent to group members.

Altruism is defined here as freely giving of oneself to others without expectations of reciprocity. Many group leaders engage in altruistic acts each time they lead groups. They do not expect group members to give back to them, but are hoping that what they give will be helpful. Leaders do not expect appreciation, compliments, acquiescence, gratitude, or total agreement, or anything similar from group members. This stance is one of the reasons why leaders can better tolerate resistance, transference, defensiveness, and projections. They are able to give and let the recipient decide what to do with what was given. Group members can learn the benefits of being altruistic from what the leader teaches and models.

Hope as a therapeutic factor is essential for group members to continue striving in the face of adversity, constraints, barriers, and setbacks. Group leaders have two primary tasks with hope. The first is to help group members frame realistic expectations, and the other is to reassure them about what is possible and that the leader can guide them in this endeavor. Hope, for some, is also provided by seeing others get better or improve and that can be another reason for the group leader to identify and openly recognize incremental progress that members achieve. I like to think of hope as rays of light or sunshine on a cloudy gloomy day, and you may have your own metaphor for hope. Try the following exercise with your group members either in a session or during the screening process.

Exercise 6.1 Visualizing Hope

Materials: Pen, pencil, and crayons; paper; a hard surface to write or draw on.

Procedure:
Ask group members to write about or draw an image of how hope appears to each of them at this moment. Once the group has completed the writing or drawing, go around the group and ask each member to read his or her written response, to elaborate on his or her drawing, and to pay attention to the thoughts, ideas, and feelings that emerged during the process and while discussing it.

Many open groups are usually formed around a common concern or issue, and these typically carry some *existential concerns* that can overtly or covertly emerge in the group. It is very helpful and facilitative when the group leader can assist group members to openly express these concerns. For example, in a group formed around a chronic medical condition, members can fear death but will resist the topic because the very thought is too overwhelmingly threatening. They can express the importance of the topic in indirect ways such as describing the session or group as "dead," resisting becoming involved and acting dead in the group, talking about the death of others but doing so without any recognition of their own mortality, and so on. Group leaders must stay aware of how the topic is of concern whether or not it is expressed openly or not, and of its many disguised forms.

A common existential issue that can emerge in open groups is the meaning and purpose for one's life. While these are individually determined, the topics can be a discussion during group sessions, or interwoven throughout many sessions. Some aspects of meaning and purpose, or the lack of them, can emerge as comments and concerns about:

- Satisfying and enduring relationships—usually the lack of these;
- Purposeful and meaningful works or other projects;
- Spirituality whether religious based or not;
- Creative endeavors;
- A sense of accomplishment.

Discussions can help group members clarify their visions of meaning and purpose for their lives, tap their inner resources of resilience, hardiness, a fighting spirit, and determination which can be immensely helpful in addressing and coping with the concern or issue that brought that member to the group. The primary point is that the group leader needs to have an awareness that the existential factor is likely to emerge and to have the ability and willingness to use it for members' growth, development, and healing.

Another facilitative strategy is to plan in advance to have and use a variety of ways to help members express their feelings. Expecting only verbal expression of feelings may not be very realistic as many people are unused to openly expressing their feelings, some feelings like guilt or shame are denied or avoided and expressing them is too threatening for the person. Expressing feelings may have been taboo in the family of origin and is now an integral part of that person, or members may not have the words for their feelings, and other such reasons. Whatever the

Exercise 6.2 Emotional Expression Activities

Materials: pens, crayons, colored pencils, felt markers, and paper; a hard surface to work on.

Procedure:

1. Express It in Writing: Select an emotion such as fear, and have members quickly write all of the thoughts, feelings, and ideas that come to mind or are associations for him or her as the group reflects on the identified feeling. These lists are then shared in the group and can be explored for better understanding of the reactions, and why it can be difficult to express that emotion.

2. Draw an Emotional Expression: Ask group members to draw a symbol or picture of a designated feeling such as anger or love. Each member then presents his or her drawing to the group and describes its personal meaning.

3. Act Out a Feeling: Select a feeling such as sadness or joy, and tell the group members to take turns and nonverbally act out the selected feeling, or act out a personal association for the feeling. Example: if joy was selected, the person could jump up with a smile and fling out his or her arms, or throw the arms up as if indicating a touchdown.

reason, it is helpful to use more than one mode for identifying or expressing these feelings.

Some techniques that can be used as well as planned in advance are writing, drawing, and acting. An example for each follows with additional such activities in chapter 12.

● ● ● ● ●

Managing Difficult Behaviors

It would be an unusual and rare group that did not experience what are generally termed as problem behaviors. These behaviors are problems because of their impact on other group members and on the group's progress and process. Problem behaviors include storytelling, monopolizing, being persistently silent or withdrawn; rejecting all assistance while at the same time complaining about not being helped; and chronic tardiness or absenteeism. Leaders of all groups need to be prepared for these behaviors to emerge and to know strategies that could effectively address them. Some examples follow.

Storytelling

Storytelling can be valued by group members in the beginning stages of a group because this provides a focus for group members, and also prevents them from having to disclose or work on their issue or concern. Also, there is the social convention about listening and showing interest that can cause many members to tolerate this ineffective behavior. Storytellers usually want others to fully understand the situation, and so they provide unnecessary details. When other members add to the story by asking questions under the mistaken perception that doing so is a way of showing interest, this keeps that person in the spotlight longer and focuses on content. If the goal of the storyteller is to be understood, then it is more facilitative to hear and respond to that person's feelings rather than asking to be given more content, such as details. Further, you do not need details to understand the storyteller's feelings, nor do you need to understand the actions of others involved in the situation, so the story that is told is hearsay, one person's perception, which could be flawed.

Following are some facilitative strategies: focus on feelings, block, interrupt, and link.

Focus on the Speaker's Feelings

1. Block questions and ask group members to respond with their personal reactions, feelings, or to reflect the speaker's feeling(s).
2. Interrupt the story and ask the speaker to report on feelings in and about the situation, and feelings aroused as the speaker tells the story in the group.
3. Interrupt the story or wait for a pause and give an empathic response.
4. Block members' attempts at advice giving or trying to "fix" the member.
5. Keep the group's focus on the storyteller and don't allow other group members to join in and start telling their stories, or if their stories are similar and relevant, try to bring the focus back to the original storyteller.

Monopolizing

Monopolizing can be difficult to address because the person may not perceive the behavior as monopolizing but be more apt to see it as being responsive, trying to help, and making a contribution. People who monopolize can be oblivious to their impact on other group members. Group leaders and members value responsiveness and contributions because these can be constructive for the group. And, there are times, such as when there is a prolonged silence in the group, where members and maybe the leader will be grateful that someone breaks the silence and provides a focus for the group. It could be more helpful to explore the meaning of the silence, but group members can be reluctant to do this. There is another explanation for the monopolizing behavior: speaking out loud helps that person to organize his or her thoughts. Whatever the reason or goal for the behavior it can be unhelpful and unconstructive. Some facilitative strategies follow:

1. The leader can point out to group members that they are letting the monopolizer do much of the work for the group.
2. If or when the therapeutic relationship has been established, the leader can interrupt and say that other members should have an opportunity

to respond, or directly ask other members for their responses, being sure to thank the monopolizer for his or her input.

3. The leader can stay aware if the monopolizer starts to veer off into storytelling and block that behavior.

4. Link the feelings expressed indirectly or directly by the monopolizer to those that were disclosed previously by other group members.

5. Some monopolizers can also be overbearing, loud, bombastic, and overly confident that they have the answers others need. In these cases, the leader is faced with a person whose personality may not be suitable or constructive for the group and may need another kind of experience. In this case, the leader needs to gauge the impact of that person's behavior on the group and consider helping him or her find a more appropriate experience. If implemented, the action should also be processed by the group.

Silence/Withdrawn

Persistent silence or being withdrawn is usually minimized by that person as being shy, needing to have time to become comfortable before becoming involved, or wanting to listen and observe, any or all of which can be true but are not helpful to the group's functioning or relationships. In addition, other members can become irritated at that member's lack of responding and disclosing; or fantasize that the silence signals judgmental thoughts about others, especially negative judgments, disapproval, the person feeling superior to other group members, and other such negative thoughts and feelings. At some point, members may turn on the silent person and begin to challenge him or her to explain or become involved, and the group leader has to be ready to intervene to prevent these challenges from becoming attacks or scapegoating that person. Facilitative strategies include prevention, especially noticing the member's silence over several sessions, and inviting his or her input. Other facilitative strategies include the following:

1. Specifically asking for that member's input or reactions. This doesn't have to take place every time or always, but at least once a session.

2. When challenged by other members, the leader can comment about the value of hearing all perspectives, reactions, and the like, but also respecting others' decisions about when or if to offer their input.

3. Discuss the level of safety and trust in the group at different times in the life of the group, and ask the group what can be done to increase these for members.

4. The leader must be aware when language difficulties may be producing the silence. For example, when English is the second language for that member, he or she may need time to mentally translate and

understand what was said before formulating a response, and that takes time so that quite often by the time he or she has a response, the other group members will have moved to another topic. When language may be a cause for silence as described here, the leader has to slow the discussion down sometimes so that this member can also provide input.

Help-Rejecting

A great deal of time and energy is spent by the group on the member who seeks but rejects assistance, the chronic complainer; and there is little to show for the efforts. No suggestion seems feasible to this person and he or she persists in bringing up the same problem or dilemma and asking for help over several sessions. Members try to provide answers, but none seems to fit, and so the frustration builds on both sides.

A group leader can prevent some of the members' frustration by limiting advice-giving behavior. Sure, members want to help, but advice is seldom welcomed or fits the particular situation. What works or seems feasible from one person's perspective is not usually directly transferable to another person's situation or personality. When members start to engage in advice-giving, the leader can intervene and acknowledge their willingness to try and help but also to point out that it would be much more helpful to provide empathic responses or report on the feelings experienced as they listen to the person. When members can do either or both, they convey understanding to the speaker about his or her feelings about the dilemma. Limiting advice giving in this matter can also be encouraging and supportive, which can contribute to that person finding his or her own solution. The adage to remember is that just as you cannot change another person, you also cannot provide the solution for another person. This can be especially true in therapy where the solution is best when it fits the solution seeking person.

Tardiness and Absenteeism

Chronic tardiness and absenteeism negatively impact the group in many ways. The leader and members are often in the dark wondering if or when this member or members will show up to session(s). Time can be lost in waiting, in trying to bring them up to date so that they feel informed, group issues and concerns may not be addressed or worked on when a member or members are missing because they played a major role, other members can feel devalued or minimized as unimportant because of the attention they draw, and other such outcomes. Many open groups can expect inconsistent attendance but that does not lessen the impact on the group and its functioning. While the group leader may be emotionally and cognitively prepared for inconsistent attendance, group members are not and can have negative reactions when members are absent, although these reactions may not be verbalized or may even be suppressed. Members may not comment on the chronic tardiness or absenteeism, which may even be excused or rationalized, but the leader should be alert to the probably disguised impact.

Group leaders may not want to comment on the tardiness or absenteeism for fear of "putting someone on the spot," or potentially embarrassing that member. However, it could also be important to bring the behavior and impact to the attention of the group and hold a discussion. Doing so can be done in a manner that attends to the possible embarrassment of that member who is chronically late or absent, using the following procedure. The example is focused on chronic tardiness:

1. Affirm the relationship and value of that member, such as saying "Sara, I noticed that you are often late and, the group does not feel complete for me until you are here."
2. Verbalize the impact on you such as, "So, when you are late I'm reluctant to begin the work as I don't want to get too far into the work and then have to stop and brief you so that you can join in the work. This really presents a dilemma for me."
3. Allow the member to respond.
4. Block other members' responses that can seem to blame or criticize the member.
5. Do not belabor the point.
6. Reaffirm the relationship, such as "I'm pleased when you join us as I value your input."

There are other basic facilitative techniques and strategies useful in other types of group that apply to open groups. These were presented in chapter 3. As noted in the beginning of this chapter, the leader's mental and emotional preparation for the vagaries of open groups are essential and crucial both to lessen the frustration and other negative emotions leaders can experience, and to increase positive outcomes for group members.

7

• • • • •

Leaderless Groups: Challenges, Benefits, and Self-Help Groups

The many different types of leaderless groups found in the literature are discussed in this chapter, with a brief summary of the research and the benefits of and constraints on these groups. In addition, self-help and support groups are very prevalent today, and this chapter has a section that addresses these groups.

• • • • •

Types of Leaderless Groups

Four major types of leaderless groups are described in the literature; expert available, self-directed, alternate session, and process- or task-oriented. The expert available leaderless group meets without a formal leader, but the "expert leader" is readily available, such as described by Seligman and Desmond (1975) where the expert leader was behind a one-way mirror. One variation of the expert leader leaderless group is when an expert is available for consultation, but not necessarily on the premises when the sessions are conducted.

Some self-directed groups defined in the literature did not have a formal or designated leader, but were guided by audiotapes, instrumented feedback, or directed instruction (Desmond & Seligman, 1977). Examples of these types are as follows:

■ Manualized minilectures, role play (Rothaus, Morton, Johnson, Cleveland, & Lyle, 1963);

■ Process—eight exercises for eight sessions (Vicino, Krussell, Deci, & Landy, 1973);

■ Peer encounter tapes (Hurst, Delworth, & Garriott, 1973);

- Caged-In (Controlled Audiotape Group Experience for Directing Individual Naturalism) (Rubenstein, 1970);

Bollet (1971), Simons (1971), Becker (1970), Taylor (1972), and Vail (1970) (as cited by Gruner, 1984) also describe self-directed groups for a variety of participants. Self-help groups are another variation of self-directed groups and are described later in this chapter.

Alternate session leaderless groups are not truly leaderless because a formal leader performs all leader tasks except that the leader only facilitates alternate group sessions (Salzberg, 1967; Seligman & Sterne, 1969; Truax & Volksdorf, 1970; Truax, Wargo, Carkuff, Kodman, & Moles, 1966). These are described here because the results presented in the literature point to some positive outcomes for some groups during the sessions where the leader is absent. There are both positive and negative aspects and outcomes for this type of leaderless group.

Process or task oriented leaderless groups are usually composed of professionals who meet to expand their knowledge and expertise in their profession through case discussion and other such presentations and are peer conducted. They may also take the form of peer supervision, and some may also function as a support for current personal concerns such as the one described by Counselman (1991).

● ● ● ● ●

Background and Literature

There are very few studies on leaderless groups other than self-help groups, and none in the past 40 plus years that used an experimental or quasi-experimental research design that incorporated a control group. Further, earlier studies with experimental or quasi-experimental designs had different outcome measures, which makes it difficult or impossible to compare the results. Most studies of all kinds tended to use participants' self-reports and lacked follow-up to determine if measured or reported changes persisted over time.

Desmond and Seligman (1977) conducted a review of the research on leaderless groups and described the major variables related to positive outcomes for leaderless groups as the:

- Group members and the issue or concern being addressed;
- Type of leaderless group and the structure and feedback provided;
- Outside the group environment for the group members; that is, institutionalized or not institutionalized.

Their review concluded that leaderless groups had more positive outcomes when the group members were "young, intelligent, and did not have serious psychological problems" (p. 19). Studies with the most positive outcomes used college students as group members. Positive outcomes were also found for groups that are highly structured and used programmed materials such as tapes and manuals. More positive outcomes were found for noninstitutionalized group members, although some positive outcomes were found when the institutionalized group members received considerable professional support services, and positive and supportive attitudes from professionals and staff at the institution.

Counselman (1991) discusses the long-term leaderless group and provides a list of leader tasks that are assumed by group members and dynamics that contribute to the healthy functioning of the group. The discussion also presents examples of long-term leaderless groups that were disbanded, and how the leader tasks and group dynamics contributed to the disbanding.

Kline (1972, 1974) described a group of psychotherapists that met over a 3-year period but disbanded when the group resisted allowing new or replacement members to join. Counselman (1991) terms this an example of how the gatekeeping leader task was not fulfilled, and there was not a clear contract about new or replacement members. Hunt and Isssacharoff (1975) also describe a group of psychotherapists who met for 3 years with the goal of case discussion. The initial purpose of case discussion was lost, personal issues and concerns became the focus, and spouses and other group members attended group sessions. That group also disbanded.

Brandes and Todd (1972) tell of yet another group of psychotherapists who met for 14 years. The group began as a peer supervision group and was disbanded when the group could not manage to contain members' problem behaviors such as absences. The group also experienced members expressing hostile feelings that produced conflicts that were not addressed or resolved. In addition to those actions and experiences, the group refused to explore the group's process and dynamics.

Two examples were presented for positive outcomes for leaderless groups. The first was a group of professional nurses who focused on peer consultation and case presentation. The second was the women's group described by Counselman (1991) that met for 17 years. The group had a requirement for participation where members were required to have engaged in personal psychotherapy. These two examples show that there can be positive outcomes for leaderless groups under certain circumstances.

● ● ● ● ●

Possible Benefits

The primary benefits for leaderless groups include the following:

■ They can be less costly both in terms of fees for participants and as payment for the leader.

■ Members may feel more empowered, self-disclose more, and take responsibility for self-healing, growth, and coping.

■ Verbal interactions among group members can be greater.

■ Members can set the agenda. This can also be true for other types of groups, but it can seem more evident to members of leaderless groups.

■ Emotional and social support are provided, as are practical applications from members' experience.

■ Isolation, alienation, or stigma related to the issue or condition are reduced.

Groups with professionally trained leaders and those financially supported by institutions, such as hospitals, are generally more costly than are other peer led leaderless groups. The costs may not be passed on to group members in some instances, and the professional's fees or salary, space, and other resources are paid for in other ways. Some leaderless groups may have membership fees, but overall these can be less. When there is a consultant leader who either attends alternate sessions or is available outside of the group, the fees for the service can be less than they would be for a leader-led group.

Leaderless groups may assist some members to feel empowered (Ahmadi, 2007), to self-disclose more (Astrachan, Harrow, Becker, Swartz, & Miller, 1967; Seligman & Desmond, 1975), and to assume some responsibility for self-healing, growth, and coping. Many of these groups are organized around a common condition, issue, or concern. The absence of a professionally trained leader who does not share the unifying purpose for the group can in itself serve to foster less dependency and encourage group members by showing them that they have many of the personal inner resources they need, that they can learn from each other, and that altruism can be enhanced by mutual support.

Members may have more verbal interaction (Holmes & Cureton, 1970; Desmond & Seligman, 1977), although the interactions may be more socially conventional (Sterne & Seligman, 1971). They may be more focused on each other than on the leader and direct their comments and responses to each other. Leaders tend to be perceived by group members as authority figures, and some members can perceive and react to leaders as parental figures (transference). In either case, when the group has a formal leader, much of the commentary is directed to and through the leader (Yalom & Leszcz, 2005). When the leader is absent, members have to take responsibility for the functioning of the group and of the sessions, and this can lead to more member to member verbal interactions.

Many leaderless groups allow group members to set the session's agenda. While there may be carryover from previous sessions, this material is not necessarily addressed in subsequent sessions as members can opt to discuss whatever seems most important and urgent for them, and this can also contribute to feelings of empowerment. The downside of member determined agendas is that sessions can wander and be directionless, which can produce feelings of dissatisfaction with the group's progress.

Most if not all leaderless groups are formed around a common concern, issue or topic, and many sessions are focused on some aspect of this commonality, such as the case presentation for nurses described by Shields and Zander (1985). Where the core purpose for the group continues to be addressed in sessions, the group accomplishes a major objective. In addition, group members have a personal connection to the commonality, and can provide emotional and social support, and will have an understanding that may not be available outside of the group. Members can better understand and some of the barriers, constraints, and challenges being encountered, and this understanding is the foundation for the emotional and social support. There is a qualitative difference between the understanding that comes from personal involvement and an external understanding of the feelings the person has but not the personal involvement with the condition or the like, as well as the challenges that produce the feelings. Both kinds of understanding are helpful and enriching, but group members can add another layer to the enrichment.

Healing, growing, and development are all enhanced when group members do not feel isolated, alienated, or weird because of the concern, issue, or condition. Knowing that others share some of the experiences, feelings, challenges, and so on can be reassuring and comforting. Group members can provide validation for each other's feelings, experiences, and the like that others in their worlds may not be able to provide. There is considerable evidence that social connections and social support are valuable resources for feelings of well-being and the group can contribute to these.

Constraints

The major constraints as presented by the literature are as follows. In the absence of a professional leader:

- There may not be screening of members regarding their suitability for the group.
- Members' problem behaviors or distress may not be monitored.
- Conflict resolution may not be modeled or implemented.
- Problem member behaviors may be ignored (e.g., monopolizing).
- Some leader tasks, such as enforcing the contract, boundaries, and rules, may not be enforced.
- Sessions may lack structure, focus, or direction.
- The out of group contract may not be honored.

Screening prospective group members is generally recommended Brown (2009), Corey (2008), and Yalom (1995). Gans and Alonso (1998) suggest that lack of screening or inadequate screening contribute to difficult members' behavior in the group. In addition to preventing negative impact on the group, its members, and the functioning of the group, screening allows the leader to determine in advance the compatibility of the person's goals with the goals, mission, and purpose for the group; his or her communication style and facility; positive and negative relating attributes; reactions to authority figures such as the leader; potential areas of sensitivity; and other personality characteristics that come into play in the group setting. However, except in rare cases, such as that described by Counselman (1991), leaderless groups do not screen potential members.

Problem member behaviors may go unrecognized or unchallenged, but can still exert a negative impact on the group. Some group leaders may leave the decision about challenging problem behaviors to the group members, but will still direct the group's attention to how the group is managing these. For example, when a member is persistently silent, the group leader usually invites input from that member, or can point out to the group the lack of inclusiveness of all group members, or in other ways draw attention to what the group is doing in respect to the silence. This is a valuable leader intervention to try and include all group members, and to prevent scapegoating or attacks on the silent member. It's not that the members of the leaderless groups are always unaware of the problem behaviors, it's either that they do not know or have the expertise to effectively manage these; they do not perceive challenging them as their responsibility, or they may be very fearful of the possible outcome such as conflict.

It is also possible that in the absence of a leader, members' distress will be ignored, minimized, or go unrecognized. This distress can be a result of something that emerged or took place in the session, or was brought into the group by that member. It really doesn't matter what the source of the distress is, but it is important that the distress is noticed and attended to in the session. Ignoring or minimizing a member's distress can send a message that the member is not valued, having distress is unacceptable in the group, and other such negative messages. Members may not know how to handle the distress, may fear the consequences of having their own distress triggered (catching others' feelings), or may just lack empathy. If distress is not attended to, this can have a negative impact on the group.

Conflict in the group can be an opportunity to learn more constructive ways to manage this, to become aware of one's usual way of behaving in conflict situations, and the extent to which this is satisfying and positive or negative, and to increase awareness of the impact on others of the various ways in which people handle conflict. When guided by a skillful group leader, members can learn conflict resolution skills which can be practiced in the group, and then carried to the members' outside lives. Leaderless groups can miss these positive outcomes, and be negatively impacted because of unresolved lingering conflicts among group members.

Other problem member behaviors, such as those described in chapter 6, can be difficult to address when there is no leader to guide group members to confront these behaviors in a way that strengthens the relationships without alienating the member who demonstrates the particular behavior. Group members are often trying to cope with their personal feelings, such as anger and frustration, may be trying to avoid conflict, or do not have the knowledge and skills for constructive confrontation. Even skilled professional group leaders can find it difficult at times to address some problem behaviors in a manner that does not blame, chastise, or in some way put the person on the hot seat, a situation that will arouse his or her defensiveness. The other side of this is that the members may not address the problem behaviors, and this can produce a situation where something very important for the functioning of the group is suppressed, denied, or ignored.

There are numerous leader tasks that are also needed for leaderless groups but, in the absence of a formal leader, may be overlooked or ignored. Leader tasks such as structuring and directing the session, enforcing or reminding the group of time boundaries or the group rules, and repairing empathic failures can be assumed by group members if they are knowledgeable about facilitating these. Other leader tasks include group process commentary, conflict resolution, constructive confrontation, assuring that members are coping adequately after intense emotional experiences, guiding the interpersonal learning through catharsis, and focusing on the underlying session's unspoken theme or members' needs. In addition to those just listed, such issues as managing resistance or understanding the impact of transference and projections on or for group members are also less likely to be addressed by group members, even when the group members themselves are mental health professionals.

Another possible constraint is that group sessions may lack structure, focus, direction, or flexibility. When members or the group as a whole resist making contact, resist intimacy or conflict, or other sensitive topics, it is unlikely that other members are knowledgeable enough to effectively address or explore them. There are also times when members may become so caught up in their own or others' stories, feelings, and the like that the focus and purpose for the session is lost, other associations emerge that can be tangential, and when explored will carry the discussion and focus even more off target. While the same situations can occur in some leader led groups, the leader is more likely to realize what is happening and bring the group's attention back to the primary focus, or is able to make a process comment that points to what the group is doing or avoiding, or in other ways keep the group from wandering. It seems that many of the reported failed or less successful leaderless groups experienced the effects of a lack of structure, direction, or focus that contributed to less effectiveness.

The final constraint discussed here is the lack of enforcement of the out of group contract. The out of group contract is usually part of the rules and expectations for group members. It specifies the parameters for interactions among group members in other settings and usually, how or when these interactions are to be reported to the group. Among the usual prohibitions can be sexual relationships, discussions of personal material disclosed by other group members during sessions, and exploration of personal material that is related to topics discussed in the group. Some groups may prohibit any social out of the group interactions among group members because these social settings can allow for inadvertent breaches of confidentiality. However, since there are some leaderless groups that are composed of colleagues, socializing out of group and other out of group contacts cannot be prohibited.

A major problem for leaderless groups can be lack of enforcement for either the out of group contract, or to bring the material discussed back to the group. The participating members in the out of group contract are responsible for notifying the group of what happened or what was discussed, and some may choose not to do so, or to feel no obligation to inform the group of this.

● ● ● ● ●

Self-Help and Support Groups

The self-help or support group is a specific type of leaderless group that is prevalent in the United States today. In 1993, Katz estimated that there were between 500,000 and 750,000 such groups with between 10 and 15 million members, and that number has increased today to over 25 million (Kessler, Mickelson, & Zhao, 1997). Ahmadi (2007) noted that these groups were also known as mutual help, mutual aid, self-help, and support groups, and that they could be described as being formed around a common problem with the mutual goals of helping members heal, recover, or cope.

There are three major types of self-help/support groups; peer facilitated, professionally facilitated, and online. Peer facilitated groups do not have a professional leader, and a major characteristic is that peers model healing for each other (Mullan, 1992). Professionally facilitated groups have a professional as the leader or as a supplemental resource (Gartner & Reissman, 1977; Kyrouz, Humphries, & Loomis, 2007). Online support groups are Web-based (Walther & Boyd, 2000). This presentation will have a primary focus on peer facilitated groups with brief descriptions provided for professionally facilitated and online groups.

● ● ● ● ●

Literature Review

Kyrouz et al. (2007) provide summaries of studies on the effectiveness of self-help mutual aid groups. They noted that many studies on self-help groups that were reported were studies of psychotherapy or support groups led by a professional only. Their review restricted the reviewed studies to peer led groups, groups that were co-led by a peer and a professional, or when the professional served as an advisor or provided other assistance. They also tried to use studies that compared group participants to a control group or to nonparticipants. The review summarized studies in several categories and, although most findings were positive, the authors did not draw any conclusions for the review.

Examples of studies reviewed included the following:

- Bereavement groups for widows and widowers (Castera & Lund, 1993; Lieberman & Videka-Sherman, 1986; Marmar & Horwitz, 1988; Vachon & Lyall, 1980);
- Bereavement for child loss (Videka-Sherman & Lieberman, 1985);

- Caregivers for the severely mentally ill (Cook, Heller, & Pickett-Schenk, 1999);

- Caregivers for the elderly (Toseland, Rossiter, & Labrecque, 1989);

- Chronic illnesses: epilepsy (Becu, Becu, Manzur, & Kochen, 1993); scoliosis (Hinrichsen & Reversol, 1985); sickle cell (Nask & Dramer, 1993); chronic pain (Subramanian, Stewart, & Smith, 1999); diabetes (Gilden & Hendrys, 1992);

- Psychiatric patients (Galanter, 1988; Kennedy, 1990; Kurtz, 1988; Powell, Hill, Warner, Yeaton, & Silk, 2000; Roberts et al., 1999).

The greatest percentage of studies reviewed was on addiction related groups such as narcotics, alcohol, and nicotine with several studies on attendance at Alcoholics Anonymous. The vast majority of these studies showed that participation in the self-help group helped to improve use/consumption, dependence symptoms, likelihood of relapse, and longer abstinence (Emrick & Tonigna, 1993; Humphreys, Mavis, & Stoffelmayr, 1994; Humphreys & Moos, 1996, 2001; McAuliffe, 1990; McKay & Alterman, 1994; Watson et al., 1997).

This review seems to show that attendees at these self-help groups used fewer professional and medical services, reported feeling less anxious, increased psychological functioning, had fewer psychosocial inferences, and had an increased positive life perspective.

● ● ● ● ●

Benefits

Among the major benefits of self-help/support groups are: empowerment; reduction of isolation; emotional, social, and practical support; learning to overcome shame and stigma; enhance self-esteem and self-efficacy; develop social skills; and provide opportunities for altruistic acts. *Empowerment* permits group members to rely more on themselves to find their personal resources to cope, grow, and heal. They can reduce feelings of dependency and take more responsibility for their own well-being. By not having a professional leader, members are encouraged and supported to make the group work. Members can become hardier, more resilient, as well as learn that they do not have to be shamed by admitting powerlessness, and to assume more control over their condition, problem, and general functioning.

Reduction of feelings of isolation is enhanced in the group process. Interacting with others, receiving encouragement and support, but most of all receiving empathic understanding of their situations contribute to feeling connected to others, and even to the universe. It is very easy to adopt feelings of isolation and alienation where you think that no one else in the world is experiencing what you are experiencing, and that you are being shoved away (isolated) because of your condition, problem, or issue.

Self-help mutual aid groups have a major purpose to provide *emotional, social, and practical support.* Members share a common concern making it easier for them to understand and to relate to each other around this commonality. They may have little else in common, but the particular condition, issue, or concern is unifying as well as being significant and important in their lives. So much can be understood among group members that does not have to be explained in detail, and it can be comforting to know that others have many of the same experiences.

Practical support is a significant contribution of the self-help/support group. This is generally provided through education, and other means to disseminate information. Indeed, some groups can have this kind of support as a structure for the sessions, and spend a significant amount of time on this support.

Borman (1992) proposes that self-help groups can aid individuals with a common condition or issue to *reduce the shame and stigma* that they may have. The group provides an opportunity to meet with others who share their experiences, to be able to interact with others without judging or being judged, learn how to cope with their feelings when others make insensitive statements or ask intrusive questions, to begin to strengthen their coping skills, and to work to educate others.

Enhancing members' self-esteem and self-efficacy can assist with providing a more positive and optimistic perspective which, in turn, helps with healing and recovery. Seeing others get better or learn to cope is a part of the group therapeutic factor of instilling hope (Yalom & Leszcz, 2005), and hope is the fuel to continue in the face of adversity. In addition, the group can provide suggestions for coping that, when tried, can also be affirming and increases self-efficacy. While the condition or issue is still present and exerting its influence, its negative effects can be reduced or eliminated.

Another of Yalom's therapeutic factors can also be a part of a self-help group by providing opportunities for socializing and for practicing socializing techniques. Members will see how others are more effective with better interpersonal relating and communication skills, and begin to adopt some of their behaviors (modeling or imitative behavior). This form of learning can be very significant and important. In addition, after some trust and safety are developed, members can begin to give each other important feedback on how they come across to others, and this can also promote some behavior changes that will make them more effective in their interpersonal relationships.

The final benefit that is discussed is the opportunity for members to participate in altruistic actions. These are defined here as freely giving to others without expecting reciprocity, and refers to nontangible gifts such as correcting misinformation and providing correct information, constructive feedback, encouragement, and support, and pointing out unrecognized strengths others may have. Following are some benefits of providing altruism found in the literature for both receivers and the givers:

- Less stress in his or her life (Cialdini, Darby, & Vincent, 1973; Midlarsky, 1991)
- Both givers and receivers report more positive life adjustment (Crandall, 1984)
- Less depression (Miller, Denton, & Tobacyk, 1986)
- Positive coping (Schwartz, Meisenhelder, Ma, & Reed, 2003)
- Better physical health (Luoh & Herzog, 2002)
- Better mental health (Schwartz et al., 2003)
- Life adaptation (Brown, Considine, & Magai, 2005)

● ● ● ● ●

Constraints

Self-help groups can have the following constraints: unmetabolized emotional contagion, group think, lack of screening, lack of a group contract or enforcement of the contract or rules, difficulty in managing intense emotions, constructive management of conflict, confrontation may not be constructive, and members may assume multiple roles both in the group and outside the group.

Hatfield, Cacioppo, and Rapson (1994) examined the research on the existence of emotional contagion and document its presence and effect in numerous situations, including in therapy. Some theorists refer to emotional contagion as poor boundary strength, projective identification, or becoming enmeshed or overwhelmed with others' feelings, and note that it can happen in many situations and interactions with others. This can be a powerful influence in the group, and have a significant effect on individual group members. I am referring to the *emotional contagion* as *unmetabolized* because of the lack of a formally trained leader who knows how to work with intense emotions and with emotional contagion. This can be important because many people are unaware that they have "caught" others' feelings which could intensify the ones they are currently experiencing, or trigger their own feelings that are usually disagreeable or unpleasant, and these can be difficult to relinquish without guidance.

Group Think is the situation that happens when a group becomes insular with an "us against them" attitude and perspective. Because of the shared and common condition or issue, the resulting feelings about this and about oneself, and the lack of understanding from others, it would not be unusual for the group members to become cohesive around their shared experience, and to feel and act as if others were in competition or were against them. This is not a good state for members to be in as it works against maintaining group relationships, and for initiating and developing other relationships.

Lack of screening for suitability for group membership can play an important role in the quality of the group experience. Yalom and Leszcz (2005) note that "it is important that the therapist screen out clients who are likely to become marked deviants in the group for which they are being considered" (p. 244), and go on to note that deviant refers to the interpersonal behavior in the group sessions, and does not refer to deviancy in lifestyle or history. Gans and Alonso (1998) also propose that many difficult member behaviors arise because of inadequate screening. Thus, screening is a significant and important group leader function, and in self-help groups without a formal leader, it is unlikely to be done.

As noted in the literature about leaderless groups, the *lack of a group contract,* especially a formal one, can be debilitating for a group. Self-help groups may suffer from the same negative outcomes when there is not a contract among members about confidentiality, out of group contact, the use of social media, and other such concerns. Considerable ambiguity and uncertainty can be reduced, and safety and trust built when members understand what is expected as well as what should not be done. When there is a group contract but that contract is not enforced, the members can feel betrayed, abandoned, angry, disappointed, and other such negative feelings. A formal group leader understands the necessity for enforcing the contract, and will bring breaches of the contract to the group even though it may be uncomfortable to do so. The absence of a formal leader may mean that the contract is not enforced, breaches go unrecognized or unaddressed, and the feelings members can have about this will be suppressed, denied, ignored, and the like.

The composition of self-help groups organized around a common concern is likely to produce *intense emotions*, and these can be difficult to cope with especially for emotionally fragile people which can be the case for some group members. Trained group leaders can help the members who are or become emotionally intense to explore the feelings to gain some insight and understanding, to help manage and contain these, and to recognize when other members may also be experiencing these, not just the speaker. It is critical that members not be allowed to leave group with intense feelings that they may not be able to manage outside the group, because these can be potentially harmful for that person's relationships, perceptions of self, and the like. While others in the group can understand the feelings, they may not be able to help manage and reduce them.

Conflict is generally present in all types of groups and is either suppressed or ignored, denied or minimized, or other such defenses are mounted to keep members from experiencing the anxiety and negative feelings that usually accompany conflict. An experienced, trained group leader can use the emergence of conflict to teach members more constructive ways to manage and resolve it, both in the group and in their other relationships. In addition, when conflict does emerge in the group, it affects all group members not just the ones actively engaged in the conflict, and a trained group leader is careful to take care of other members in addition to the active conflicted members.

● ● ● ● ●

Online Support Groups

This is a fast growing source for support groups (Ainsworth, 2008), and there are numerous reasons for this growth. Major benefits include the following:

- Participation is asynchronous as all group members do not have to be logged in at the same time.
- The social distance and anonymity reduces embarrassment.
- Comments, questions, and the like can be edited before being posted, which provides an opportunity to ensure that what is meant is what is being said.
- Participation can occur at any time.
- The Internet has been shown as helpful in giving social support for those with chronic health problems.
- The support group can be available for those in remote areas or who have schedules that would make it difficult to attend in person groups.

However, there are also some constraints. Potts (2005) notes that it can be difficult to find the appropriate group as there are no directories, some groups are not listed by search engines, and there is no oversight or means for quality control. The online groups can also contain lurkers who are people who are present and reading messages, but do not post any of their own, or let others know that they are present.

Regardless of the constraints, online support groups can provide information, social support, a venue for expressing difficult and important feelings, reduce feelings of isolation, and other positive outcomes. Much more research is needed as are guidelines for responsible conduction and use of this resource.

● ● ● ● ●

Summary

In spite of the many and important constraints, self-help groups do seem to be helpful for some people, and can provide growth and healing for participants. The positive outcomes reported in the literature, and the benefits reported by participants support the need and uses for these groups.

8

• • • • •

Leaderless Groups:
Guidelines for Facilitation

The suggestions provided in this chapter are intended to guide the use of leaderless and self-help groups so that they can be effective and safe. Since many or all of the members of such groups may not read this book, the suggestions are mainly for consultants to the group, directors or others who form such groups, and for trainers of group leaders. The guidelines for leaderless groups were formulated with the following as fundamentals, and additional guidelines for self-help groups are presented later in the chapter.

The literature about these groups is scant and may be skewed because of the lack of information. However, it seems that leaderless groups seem to work best with educated mature group members who are psychologically mature, but these groups are counterindicated for adolescents, institutionalized group members, or those with serious psychiatric pathology. The literature also seems to suggest that an educational or cognitive focus, such as case presentations, can be helpful and more successful.

• • • • •

Basic Guidelines

There are six basic guidelines:

- Establish a focus, goal, or purpose and a checkup schedule.
- Generate rules for participation and for conducting sessions.
- Develop a group contract.
- Decide group facilitation procedures.

- Secure an external consultant.
- Create an open or closed group structure.

It is highly recommended that the organizers for a leaderless group meet in advance of the first group session to carry out all of the listed tasks. If there is only one person doing the organizing, these items and the decisions made by that person should be brought to the group at the first session for their agreement and input. Modifications can be made at that time.

The benefits for a clearly stated focus, goal, or purpose for the group cannot be overstated. Why are we here, what will I get out of this experience, and what are we supposed to do are common questions members have when they enter the group either at the beginning or later. These are not unusual questions, they occur for all groups even when the questions are anticipated and answered in advance. This is just a sign of the anxiety they can have when entering a new and unknown situation.

It is very helpful when the organizers of the leaderless group agree in advance about the purpose for the group, anticipated goals, and major focus, and convey this to prospective members prior to their joining the group. Even when this is done in advance of the beginning of the group, care should be taken to restate this at the first session and obtain group members' agreement and commitment to them. It is recommended that the agreed on decisions be provided in writing. It is also recommended that the group do a goal checkup at specified intervals to assess progress, and viability of the preestablished goal. The goal or focus may change as the group progresses. The change may be intentional or unintentional. If the change is intentional, members need to collaboratively set a new goal. If the change is unintentional, such as what can happen when the group on an unconscious level has started to move in another direction, this change needs to be made visible, discussed, and agreed on as a group.

Group members feel more secure when there are known rules for participation, and when these rules are enforced. The absence of a formal leader can lead to a lack of enforcement, and this produces anxiety, ambiguity, and uncertainty. Even worse is when there is inconsistent enforcement which can produce feelings of unfair treatment. For example, suppose that the group has a rule that phones are turned off during sessions and a phone rings, the member quickly apologizes and turns it off after sneaking a glance to see who was calling, and the group continues without saying anything about the breach of the rule. However, at another session, the same thing happens with another member but members do not ignore this and say things like, "It's the rule," "I always check to make sure my phone is turned off," and other similar comments, which can cause the rule-breaking member to perceive that he or she is being treated differently and more harshly than the member who had broken the rule earlier.

Group contracts are agreements among group members about acceptable and unacceptable behavior in and out of group experiences that relate to the group. The line between contracts and rules can become blurred but think of rules as relating more to sessions, and the contract as relating more to the overall structure for conducting the group. Group contracts usually specify rules and norms. Two major difficulties with group contracts are that these are seldom written, and some portions may not be specifically stated, but are thought to be understood by all. Whether it is termed a contract or rules, these should be written and discussed among group members. Some items to be included are the following:

- Penalties, if any, for noncompliance; such as whether the offending member is allowed to continue as a part of the group, or other such actions.

- What can be talked about outside of the group even with other members of the group, or with people who are not group members.

- How and when other members can be added or replacement members for those who leave the group.

- The use of social media, what is an acceptable posting and what is not.

- Out of group contact among group members. That is, where is the line between this group as a working group with limitations on this sort of contact, and a social group with few or no limitations on social contact?

- The extent of confidentiality for personal material disclosed in sessions.

- Exchange of gifts among group members.

There are some basic group facilitation tasks that can be assumed by one or more group members that will help leaderless groups. It is helpful to decide these in advance so that there is a designated person or person who knows in advance that this will be their assigned task. These tasks can rotate among group members. Basic tasks are beginning and ending sessions on time, recapping at the end of the session any decisions made during that session, noting the absence of a group member, facilitating the standard session beginning activity such as a check-in on current feelings, introduction of a new member, and the announcement of a terminating member. These tasks can be rotated or vested in several members who will consistently perform the particular tasks, or volunteers at each session can be asked to perform the tasks at the next session.

It is important to respect time boundaries by beginning and ending on time. One characteristic of some leaderless group is inconsistent attendance so it is recommended that the start of the session not be delayed in anticipation of some possible late arrivals. Ending on time is equally as important and that is also recommended. However, in the event that a group member is in the throes of an intense emotional disclosure, it is important to finish that, but do so as quickly as possible, and indicate that the topic can be continued in the next session. If a group member brings up an important topic at or near the end of the session, ask if he or she could bring it back to the next session and not take the time to explore it at that time as the member could have introduced the topic earlier when there would have been enough time for that exploration.

Recapping decisions and assignments at the end of a session fulfills several purposes. The first is to provide a summary of what was done and will be done for the next session, it provides closure for this session, a cognitive focus can help mediate some lingering intense emotions experienced during the session, and can serve as a reminder for members who have an assignment.

Some leaderless groups are closed groups, and some are open. In either case, inconsistent attendance may occur. A trained group leader understands the importance of openly noting the absence of a group member even when the reason for the absence is not known. When a member is absent, the group is incomplete, and dynamics can or will change, and by openly speaking of the absence, other group members can understand that their presence is valued and is noticed when they are absent. Think of how someone can feel when he or she is absent, no one notices, and the absence did not seem to make a difference for the group. It's as if the absent person was of little or no consequence and was not valued. The absence may not make a huge difference, but there is some difference.

Many groups can have a standard or ritualistic beginning activity and a group member can facilitate this when there is no formal leader. After all, the standard or ritual activity is there to provide some constancy and certainty which is reassuring for many group members. Examples of beginning activities can include the following:

■ A brief silence or meditation;

■ Check-in by each member on their current condition or major events in their lives since the previous session;

- A review of the previous session;

- Asking if there is unfinished business from the previous session such as unexpressed thoughts or feelings, additional thoughts or feelings that emerged after the session, repair of empathic failures, and so on.

It is assumed that someone invites a new member to join the group, or that there is a process for bringing in the new members. However that may happen, it is important that the new member receive an introduction to the group. It is not sufficient to just have the new person provide his or her name, it is also important for other members to introduce themselves, and for both to provide some additional information as a welcome. For example, all could relate what they expect the group to personally provide for them, what motivated them to join the group, or other such group-focused information. It could be helpful to limit or not request more personal information at this time, but rather let the members decide what, when, or if to provide this information. While the group is not a social event, it could still send an important message to all that members are valued, a new member is not an additive event, the dynamics are apt to change, and that the group itself is important to its members.

A critical component for leaderless groups is the access to an outside consultant knowledgeable about the purpose for the group, and on group dynamics. It is difficult enough for a trained group leader to facilitate a group, and it is highly recommended that supervision be provided for this professional leader. Many situations arise, such as groups finding that they become stuck or mired; conflict emerges but is not resolved; cliques develop and exert a negative influence; resistance and defensiveness become barriers to the group's progress and functioning; difficult member behaviors are not addressed; and many other such situations occur. It is helpful to be able to consult with someone outside the group about possible strategies to help resolve or address these and any other distressing situations. It is highly recommended that leaderless groups have such a resource and that the person be made known to all group members, and that all members have access to him or her. While a designated person could consult on a situation with the consent of group members, in the absence of a formal group leader, it needs to be clear that anyone can consult. The person chosen has to be seen as trustworthy by group members, to have an understanding about confidentiality of material when consulted, and to be available.

● ● ● ● ●

Guidelines for Self-Help Leaderless Groups

Self-help/mutual support groups are very different from other types of leaderless groups and for that reason they are presented separately in this section. There is considerable information to guide the organizing, marketing, programming, and facilitating of these groups available on the Internet, and readers are encouraged to use those resources for the latest and most complete information. For example, when I used Google to search for sources of information, 120 million results were obtained, indicating that there are numerous resources available.

Examples of specific sources are as follows:

■ SOS guidelines for group leaders: http://www.cfiwest.org

■ Iowa State University—Guidelines for a self-help group: http://www. estension.iastate.edu/pub

■ Wichita State—Program ideas: http://www.wichita.edu/ccsr

■ National Stuttering Project: http://www.mnsu.edu/comdis/kuster/ SupportOrganizations/peercounseling.html

■ The National Multiple Sclerosis Society: *Best Practices Leaders Manual* (2010)

This chapter is limited to guidelines for group structure and facilitation. All resources consulted emphasize the need to create a safe and healthy group environment, and the sharing of responsibilities for the functioning of the group. Some common guidelines for promotion of members' disclosure, sharing, and interactions are consistent with recommended group practices for leader provided groups, and are as follows.

1. Respect anonymity and confidentiality of disclosures.
2. One person speaks at a time, and interruptions are discouraged.
3. Monitoring of speaking time for sharing concerns, stories, and the like.
4. Avoid giving advice, confronting, or putting others on the spot.
5. Share comments with the group as a whole, no cross-talk or side conversations.
6. Differences of opinion are tolerated and respected.
7. Do not diagnose, suggest a course of treatment, instruct, or act as therapists.

8. Do not discuss absent group members. What can be discussed are the members' feelings about the difference created in the group by the absence.
9. Questions may be asked, but members are not forced to answer these.

It could be very helpful for the group to discuss each of these items and come to a consensus as to what the guidelines mean for them personally because clearly there will be diverse opinions, which members need to try to operationalize. If possible, a gatekeeper could be appointed to keep track of the rules and bring it to members' attention when they are violated.

Regardless of how the leadership tasks are handled, there are some common leader tasks that each group member can undertake and facilitate:

- Understand the difficulty in trying to focus on personal issues and others in the group at the same time.
- The personal desire to help to "fix it."
- Accept that each member has the wisdom and resources within him- or herself that can be used for coping.
- Openly recognize members' strengths and resilience.
- Understand one's own personal limitations.
- Provide encouragement and support.
- Do not downplay or minimize realistic fears.
- Have an opening and closing ritual for sessions.
- Check the validity of information before it is disseminated.
- Learn to manage problem behaviors.
- Do not shame members.
- Remember the rules and apply them consistently.
- Use an outside consultant.

Group leaders must stay mindful of the possibility of subjective countertransference where their personal issues may negatively impact group members. Learning about one's unresolved issues and other unfinished business, and working to address these are considered to be an integral part of preparation as a mental health professional, and are especially important for group leaders who will be dealing with multiple individuals in the group, and can have their countertransference triggered at any time. It is very difficult to focus on personal issues and those of others at the same time, and the leaders/facilitators for leaderless and self-help/support groups may find this to be a particular challenge.

Group leaders, whether formally trained or not, want to help group members to grow, develop, heal, and get better and can expend considerable effort to accomplish this. The difficulty can be that this desire to fix whatever is perceived as in need of fixing, can lead the leader to participate in some ineffective behaviors, such as pushing for a disclosure, trying to break down resistance, or advice giving. These actions can be destructive although the motive is commendable. Worse can be when the group leader fails to block other group members from these actions which can also be harmful. Group leaders need to take their cues from group members about the amount and level of self-disclosure, leave resistance alone, wait for the person to feel comfortable lowering his or her defenses, and refrain from giving advice, which is seldom appreciated or fits that person. It is much more helpful to give and encourage group members to give empathic responses, and to be respectful of resistance.

Adopt an attitude that each group member has the wisdom and inner resources that will help that person cope, and work from that perspective. Rather than providing answers, provide hope and encouragement by showing that you have faith in their ability to help themselves, and that the group and leader are there to guide them to finding their personal wisdom and becoming aware of their inner resources that are not being used, indeed of which they are not aware.

Recognize the strengths and resilience that group members may not recognize or may minimize by openly acknowledging these as you observe the members. There are times when individuals focus more on their weaknesses, deficiencies, and the like, than they do their strengths and examples of resilience. There can be remedial work that needs to be done, but the most positive and successful work comes from capitalizing on strengths.

The leader's desire to be helpful, successful, and effective can lead to frustration when personal limitations are not understood. For example, it is impossible to fully understand another person, to change someone, or to prevent them from self-destructive behaviors, and if these limitations are not fully accepted, leaders can become depressed, discouraged, and even angry at self and at others.

Members in all types of groups can benefit from encouragement and support, but in self-help groups these can be even more important. Members who are undergoing adversity need some external validation of their circumstances, and expressions of faith in their abilities to cope, grow, and heal. Peer group leader can be mindful of this need, and use encouraging and reinforcing statements that recognize the member's efforts.

Expressions of fears can produce discomfort for others, and many responses can tend to minimize the fear, or suggest that it is irrational. However, when people are attending a self-help group, they are likely to have some realistic fears about their ability to cope, how their lives and relationships will change, prognosis for the future for healing, recovery, repair, and return to better functioning, and other such concerns. It is important for the group leader and other members to accept the fear as a realistic one, to not try to get away from the fear because of the inability to make things better or to fix it, or because it is reflective of his or her own unexpressed fear. It is much more helpful to acknowledge the possibilities, to explore ways to keep the fear from paralyzing the person, or explore what the individual can do in realistic terms to help him- or herself, and what other associations they may have for that fear.

It can be comforting for members to establish a ritual for opening and closing of sessions as they come to know what will be expected. The opening ritual helps them to become integrated into the group session again, and the closing ritual provides them with an opportunity to get ready to transition to the world outside of the group. It's been mentioned before that check-ins and meditations are common opening rituals. The group may suggest or develop its own unique ritual. Closing rituals can be summaries, asking members for one thing they learned or will take away from the session, or a moment of silence as closure.

It is essential to check the validity of any information that is to be disseminated to the group, especially the source of the information. It is amazing that numerous well-educated and intelligent people can believe that because information was retrieved from Internet sources that the information has to be valid and correct. Nothing can be further from the truth. There are considerable misinformation, distortion, and even lies on the Internet. In addition, not everything you read or hear is accurate either. Check the validity and credibility of the sources for any information. It is recommended that experts who are knowledgeable about the topic be used as consultants for this task.

9

• • • • •

Single Session Groups: Challenges and Benefits

Single session groups will be discussed from two perspectives: the planned group that will have only one session and the group where one or more members only attend one session although the group is scheduled for further sessions. In short, the members prematurely terminate their group experience. The planned single session group is known from the start by the leader and the members to have a limited life span. The other situation is unplanned by the leader, and may be unplanned by the member, and is unanticipated and member specific. The unplanned single session group is encountered more often that may be thought. Baekeland and Lundwall (1975) found that 20 to 57% of clients terminate after the first session, making this a significant concern for group leaders.

Planned single session groups tend to be focused on education, skills training, work-related topics, or brief introductions to a therapeutic strategy. These groups have a narrowly defined goal, are usually very structured, a significant amount of time is devoted to teaching and dissemination of information, and they vary in the amount of time allotted for that single session. Examples for planned single session groups are workshops, training groups, presentations, and seminars for small groups where there is expected member interaction and participation, and demonstrations for a technique or skill.

Unplanned single session groups are defined here as those groups where one or more members terminate the group after one session. This is usually termed *premature termination*, the group or group leader is not notified of the intent to not continue attending, which presents a dilemma for the leader and the remaining group members. Hall (2012) found that there are various definitions for premature termination, especially for groups where members attend more than one session, but terminate before the planned ending of the group. The following models are presented as possible explanations for premature termination which are intended to help leaders and group members to understand and thereby reduce or eliminate fantasies about what may have occurred in the group that led to the member leaving without notice, and to also prevent self- or other blame, criticizing, and maybe even guilt feelings.

● ● ● ● ●

Models for Premature Termination (PT)

Hall (2012) describes three primary models for premature termination: the behavioral model of health services use (Andersen, 1968/1995a); the barriers to treatment model (Kazdin, Holland, & Crowley, 1997; Kazdin & Wassell, 2000); and the delay discounting model (Swift & Callahan, 2010).

The behavioral model (Andersen, 1968/1995b) has three categories: primary determinants of health behavior, health behavior, and health outcomes. The primary determinants of health utilization behavior are population characteristics, the health care system, and the external environment. Population characteristics are those such as race, age, gender, culture, social network, social interaction, education, occupation, and ethnicity; beliefs, attitudes, values, and knowledge of health; genetic factors; the individual's status in the community; available resources such as money, social networking, health insurance; the ability to cope with problems; and psychological issues such as cognitive deficits, mental dysfunction, and autonomy. The health care system includes the organizational/systemic influences on health policy, availability of health resources in the community, and health policy changes over time. The external environment describes physical characteristics of the environment such as the setting, crime rates, political influences, and economic variables.

The second category, health behavior, includes personal health practices and use of health care services. Personal health practices are behaviors such as diet, exercise, and self-care. The use of health care services refers to the type of health care services accessed, the setting, and the reason for seeking services.

Health seeking outcomes is composed of perceived and evaluated health status. Perceived health status refers to the extent to which professionals and the public agree that public health is effective; and evaluated health status refers to the satisfaction that there is effective access to needed services and consumer satisfaction.

The barriers-to-treatment model was developed as a conceptual tool for researchers to aid in understanding and predicting PT. This model proposes that therapy may be viewed by clients as an inconvenient and demanding task (Kazdin & Wassell, 2000); and that clients who encounter barriers report that this inhibits their motivation (Kazdin et al., 1997). Three general barriers are: structural barriers, perceptions about mental health problems, and obstructive perceptions about mental health services (Owens et al., 2002). Structural barriers are external obstacles that prevent access to treatment; such as a lack of health insurance, inadequate coverage, a lack of qualified providers, transportation difficulties, unreasonable service costs, and difficulties in accessing services. Perceptions about mental health problems are internally held attitudes by the individual that may limit or prevent access to treatment services; these attitudes may take the form of minimizing the problem, failing to recognize that they have a diagnosable mental health problem, and faulty perceptions about their personal ability to control mental health symptoms. Obstructive perceptions about mental health services describe negative beliefs about treatment, such as previous negative experiences and social stigma (Owens et al., 2002).

Baekeland and Lundwall (1975) found that approximately 20 to 57% of clients drop out after the initial session and between 31 and 56% withdraw before completing four visits. Phillips (1987) reported evidence from the literature suggesting that the mean number of sessions attended is 4.7. Further evidence suggests that between 27 and 70% of clients report marked improvements between 1 and 3 months of treatment, and another 18% report marked changes between 4 and 6 months of psychotherapy treatment. Phillips (1987) concluded that the termination rate was an unstable factor.

The *delay discounting model* uses the devaluation of an outcome as a motivation for premature termination (Green et al., 2004; Swift & Callahan, 2010). When clients are faced with either accepting the current outcome or deciding to continue for the potentially greater outcome, delay discounting represents the decision to choose between a smaller but current reward versus a potentially greater reward to be found in the future outcome. Evidence for the delay discounting model is seen from studies that show that the median number of sessions attended is about six and, as the length of treatment increases, the number of clients who continue in therapy falls (Garfield, 1978, 1994).

Pekarik (1985) also suggests that clients may settle for a modest level of improvement and may refuse longer treatment even when that is recommended by the therapist (Garfield, 1978, 1994; Pekarik, 1985). These findings suggest that clients may terminate early because they perceive that they have made acceptable gains in treatment and think that further therapy is unnecessary.

● ● ● ● ●

Benefits

At first glance, single session groups can appear to be so limiting that their value is minimal at best. After all, growth, development, and healing take time and effort as well as considerable self-exploration and understanding that also require time. There is no contest between the benefits of numerous sessions over a single session but there are some positive things that can be achieved.

There are at least seven possible benefits for single session groups, both planned and unplanned:

- Receive information;
- Provide an opportunity for expression of feelings;
- Generate new ideas;
- Become inspired;
- Receive attention for concerns and feelings;
- Can provide consensual validation;
- Practice a skill.

Receive Information

Although it is a given that a single session is likely to be insufficient for many concerns, issues, problems, or for learning a complex skill, there are some positive outcomes for the members who only attend one session. Receiving information is a benefit that should not be underestimated or discounted. Regardless of the issue, concern, or need that is the focus for the group, learning is an integral part of almost every group. The information received does not have to be considerable or formally presented, but the group leader should plan to have some information presented at every session when the group is planned to be more than one session, and not intend that the new information has to be built on previous information; that is, the new information should be capable of standing alone. If the group is planned to be only one session, presenting information is a planned part of that group.

The basic idea is that every member, including the member who will only attend one session (although is not known in advance), should receive some information that could be helpful. This member may decide to prematurely terminate, but will leave with a piece of information that he or she did not have before the single session.

Express Feelings

Group sessions can provide an opportunity for members to more freely express their feelings, especially their intensely negative ones. It may also be that these members have no other forum or safe place where these feelings can be openly voiced without censure. While simple venting does not produce insight or learning, it can provide some measure of relief. It can be important for the group leader and members to be accepting of these feelings and not try to minimize or ignore them, or in any way suggest that the feelings are wrong. Leaders and members don't have to agree that the feelings are justified, but neither should they express disapproval. It would be helpful if that member would return to the group and work on the issues and feelings, but that does not always happen so that the moment that the member does express some feelings should be capitalized on by simply listening, reflecting the meaning(s), and providing the member with an empathic response.

Generate New Ideas

Many members can be in turmoil when attending the group, especially at the first session where they have the usual concerns about being helped, included, understood, and can be apprehensive about what is expected of them: Is the group safe, can the leader and other group members be trusted, and so on. There is so much swirling around in their minds, and there could also be multiple and conflicting feelings that prevent clear thinking. The members can be so mired in their misery that they cannot envision how they can find the help they are seeking. But, even in the first meeting, the group has the potential to help members generate new ideas, such as:

- Different ideas about the condition, issue, or concern that brought them to the group that could be helpful;
- Other sources of help that could be tapped;
- How to access their inner resources of resilience, hardiness, determination, and the like;
- More effective ways to communicate and relate;
- Increase the meaning and purpose for their lives;
- Better coping or problem solving strategies.

Developing even one new idea can make that session worthwhile for that group member.

Become Inspired

Inspiration can happen at any time and can come from many sources. While it is difficult to predict what is inspiring for anyone, group leaders can plan for positive activities, interventions, and the like as an integral part of every session. Central to the idea of providing inspiration for the group is the group leader's ability to model the following: faith in the group and in members that they have the resources needed to grow, develop, and heal; an awareness of members' strengths that can be emphasized; an understanding of the importance of encouragement and support and the willingness to provide these; and a realistic appraisal and acceptance of oneself as valued and worthwhile. Group members can also provide inspiration, but that cannot be planned. However, the group leader can capitalize on these when they do occur by highlighting them and their positive aspects. Examples of contributions members can make include the following:

- Reporting to the group on positive changes they implemented and the feelings they have about the outcomes and their sense of self-efficacy.
- Describing their progress toward desired goals.
- Identifying positive aspects of their self.
- Illustrative reports of overcoming adversity and other barriers or setbacks.
- Any improvements in their relationships or conditions.
- Receiving or giving feedback on unrecognized strengths.
- Performing altruistic acts both in and out of the group.

Inspiration can provide a measure of realistic hope that can be very helpful.

Receive Attention

The group is a place where members can receive attention for their concerns and feelings. These can be expressed, explored, and can receive empathic responses. The attentive and responsive group leader does not discount, overlook, minimize, or try to get away from these because of the intensity of the concerns and the feelings they arouse. Group members may not experience this level of attention and caring in their everyday lives. Some may be alone without family or other social support, some may not have family relationships that are constructive and satisfying, and other such personal situations. This lack of acceptance, caring, concern, and empathic responding in their everyday lives can be especially acute if the member's condition, concern, or issue is chronic and complex. Others can feel helpless to fix it or make it better, and so they withdraw and the affected person does not get the attention and responses that could be helpful.

The commonalty that members have in the group around an issue can provide additional support and encouragement as well as attention because of the shared situation or experiences. Other members can understand at a deeper level some of the feelings and other experiences each member expresses and respond empathically. The group provides a climate where attention to members is expected unlike many other places outside of the group such as among family, colleagues, and friends where attention can be brief or even nonexistent. Some attention reassures that the person is valued and validates the situation or concern.

Consensual Validation

Consensual validation refers to the agreements among group members that feelings, experiences, reactions and so on are real and are shared. This validation reduces isolation, feelings of being different or alienated, and fears of having deep character flaws that cannot be "fixed" and are shaming. These states are difficult to endure and are rarely spoken of, but can have negative and lasting effects on the individual's self-esteem, relationships, and general functioning. The realization that others share feelings and experiences can be inspiring and comforting.

Learn and Practice New Skills

The group can provide opportunities to learn and practice new skills, and group leaders could plan to introduce a different skill each session, such as various communication and relating skills. The introduction of the skill does not need to be formal or structured, but can be an informal presentation and an opportunity to practice a new skill. Examples for possible new skills include the following:

- Practicing nonverbal attending skills, such as orienting the body toward the speaker or maintaining eye contact;
- Learning to accept compliments without disclaimers or self-disparagement;
- Listening for feelings;

- Naming or labeling one's feelings instead of expecting others to intuit these;
- Responding directly and concretely to others;
- Respectful assertion;
- Recognizing empathic failures.

Here are two examples for skill building activities/exercises.

Exercise 9.1 Making Connections

Materials: A preprinted sheet with the following items for each group member and a pen or pencil for each.

Procedure:
Instruct group members to find the group member who shares an interest in each of the following, write the specific interest in the designated space, such as football for sports, and the name of the person who shares your interest. Distribute the materials and explain the exercise. Ask members to talk to each member separately and see if there is a commonality of interest. Allow about 10 to 15 minutes to complete this portion. After members resume their seats in the group circle, ask them to share their commonalties, and then ask what it was like to do the exercise, such as, "What feelings were aroused as you talked with other group members?"

	Specifics	Person(s)
Sport	_____	_____
TV show	_____	_____
Kind of music	_____	_____
Reading material; e.g., magazines, books	_____	_____
Type of food; e.g., a dessert	_____	_____

Exercise 9.2 Immediate Feelings

Materials: A sheet of paper, a set of crayons or felt markers for each group member, and a hard surface suitable for drawing.

Procedure:
Distribute the materials and explain the exercise as follows: "Each of you brought some feelings to the session. Think of three feelings you have at this moment or had as the group began. Select a different color for each feeling and draw a symbol for each of the three feelings. The symbol can be realistic or abstract, whatever you choose."

Allow 10 to 15 minutes for the drawing. Reconvene in the group circle, share the drawings with as much explanation of the symbols as the member wishes to present. After each member has an opportunity to share, ask them to report on the thoughts, feelings, and ideas they experienced as they thought of the feelings they brought to the group and as they shared in the group.

There are many such skills that with practice could be minilessons. This way, even when someone attends one session, there is the possibility that he or she gains something positive as a result of attending the session.

It is helpful when the group leader can have a balanced perspective for either planned or unplanned single session groups, and can focus on both the benefits and the constraints. Group members can tune into the leader's feelings and mood on a nonconscious level, and may also unconsciously adopt these and act on them. Recognizing that there is something positive that can be gained from a single session can provide hope and encouragement for all involved.

● ● ● ● ●

Constraints

The constraints for single sessions are primarily related to the lack of sufficient time for many group and therapeutic factors to appear or to unfold. Group factors such as trust and safety, developing relationships among group members and with the leader, learning to give and receive constructive feedback, constructive management of conflict, and other such factors need time to emerge, and a single session may not be sufficient.

Yalom and Leszcz's (2005) therapeutic group factors such as imitative behavior, socializing techniques, catharsis with interpersonal learning feedback loop, the corrective recapitulation of the primary family group, existential factors, and group cohesiveness are less likely to emerge and be worked on in a single session. These are therapeutic group factors that need time to emerge or be fostered, to be recognized and addressed, and for personal associations or connections to be made by all or most group members.

The group leader can be keenly aware that a single session does not provide enough time for group members to explore their reactions, personal associations, resistances, defenses, feelings that are triggered, or to generate complex ideas or practice complex skills. The richness of experiencing that comes with longer term groups is limited or nonexistent. These losses can produce considerable leader frustration.

In some ways, the group leader's frustration and feelings of futility are a major constraint because these can prevent him or her from more fully capitalizing on constructive use of the time that is available. Leaders who are more attuned to what cannot be done miss opportunities to make the single session as productive as it could possibly be if the focus and attitude were on what can be done, and have a sense of satisfaction and accomplishment for the limited outcomes. It would be much more beneficial for the group and for the leader to take pride and be joyful for the modest or minimal amount of work that is done.

● ● ● ● ●

Planned Single Group Sessions

Rather than fret about what cannot be done for a single session, it is more rewarding and helpful to capitalize on the opportunities that are available. For example, a planned single session could be conceived of as a workshop where group members will be introduced to one new skill, such as problem solving, and have an opportunity to personalize and practice that skill. The focus and emphasis for the session has the skill as the subject matter, and all activities are geared toward that single topic; the introductory exercise, information to be presented, and the selection of activities. An added advantage may be that all group members do not have the same problem, but all can learn from the process, such as learning a procedure and process for problem solving. An additional advantage of this approach can be that it gives the member of a planned longer term group who may prematurely terminate in the future, some valuable understanding, knowledge, and skill.

This conceptualization for single group sessions for planned multisession groups is to make each session self-contained (Brown, 2011). Thus, each session need not necessarily build on the previous one(s), although that is desirable and recommended, but can stand alone in its intent, goals, purpose, and strategies. This approach uses a realistic perspective to provide group members with some measure of knowledge, skill, hope, and the like that can be helpful and useful in their lives outside of the group. A process for planning single sessions and self-contained sessions for groups having planned multisessions is in chapter 10.

Following is a list of possible general topics for planned single sessions:

■ Problem-solving/decision-making

■ Time management

- Conflict resolution
- Managing and containing difficult and unpleasant feelings
- Appropriate expression of feelings
- Consultation
- Supervision
- Performance evaluation
- Team development
- Providing constructive feedback

10

● ● ● ● ●

Single Session Groups: Planned or Unplanned Groups, Managing Premature Termination

There are many variations for the planned single session group and unifying factors for all types are as follows:

■ Specific time boundaries are set and known in advance of the start of the group.

■ The session has a comprehensive structure.

■ There is a need to balance cognitive and affective concerns.

■ An active group leader directs the session.

■ Limited goal(s) and objectives.

■ Reduction or elimination of sequential learning over time and completion of out of group tasks.

■ Lack of time for an unfolding process, significant self-exploration for members, or establishment of a deep therapeutic relationship.

● ● ● ● ●

Time Boundaries

Planned single session groups have specific time boundaries that are usually established in advance, and group members are expected to be present for that period of time. The session is constructed to allow for a measured amount of learning and growth, and the activities and processes therein can be sequential which means that group members must be present for all aspects in order to gain maximum benefit. The time allotted for the session can vary widely from 1 to 8 hours, such as that for workshops. Group leaders establish and disseminate the time frame to group members prior to the beginning of the group as well as the explicit expectation and assumption that all members will attend for the entire time.

• • • • •

A Comprehensive Structure

Comprehensive structure indicates that the directions and activities for the entire session, including time allotted for each component, are planned in advance and this agenda is followed. Thus, planned single session groups are more highly structured and directed with much of an emphasis on completing planned tasks and activities. Generally, the target audience is known in advance so that planning will meet their needs and abilities. The group leader acts as a director, staying on task, and moving the experience along to complete the preplanned agenda. This does not mean that process or members' self-explorations are ignored because these can be planned for and time allotted. However, these are not able to be as in depth as would be possible in groups with more than one session.

• • • • •

Balance: Cognitive and Affective

The group leader must stay aware of maintaining a balance of cognitive and affective group members' needs. Both are dependent on the goals and objectives for the single session, and both should receive attention. It can be difficult to know in advance which will be most important for a particular group, what could emerge or be triggered because of the material or activities presented in the session, which could shift the emphasis or focus, or an unanticipated event that impacts group members. It is helpful for the group leader to stay aware of this need for balance and to also be flexible enough to make needed adjustments without seriously compromising the planned structure.

• • • • •

An Active Group Leader

The structuring and time constraints for single session groups demand an active leader who stays on task, enforces time boundaries for activities, invites input from each group member as well as also staying aware of other group dynamics, such as resistance and expression of feelings. Given the time frame, the usual therapeutic relationship expected in other types of groups, such as therapy groups, cannot be established, but it is portrayed in a different form in that the leader is more task than relationship focused. While there should always be time for members to engage in self-reflection, the group leader can find that there is less time for this to unfold because of the need to complete the tasks, and must find a way to encourage group members to continue that endeavor after leaving the group.

● ● ● ● ●

Limit Goals and Objectives

Limited goals and objectives are critical for single session groups as these will help keep the session focused on essentials. Goals and objectives should be realistic and, at the same time, provide for some measure of learning, growth, development, or healing. These should also be measurable and achievable so that the constraints for these types of groups do not become frustrating.

Goals, as defined above, are expected outcomes relevant to the focus and purpose for the group. These can be more easily created for task and educational groups, such as time management and parent education; and for some psychoeducational and counseling groups, such as anger management and relationship building groups. While all of these groups could benefit from longer time frames and additional sessions, they can also accomplish much in a single session.

Developing goals and objectives is presented more completely in the opening chapters, and it would be helpful to review that information when planning your single session group. An example for goals and objectives for a single session of 3 to 6 hours on conflict resolution follows. The example assumes that the group is for adults who do not know or work with each other, and that participation and attendance is voluntary.

- Goal: To learn a constructive conflict resolution procedure.

- Objectives: Group members will learn and practice the following:
   1. Their usual personal conflict behavior and its impact on others, and their degree of satisfaction with the outcomes.
   2. How to recognize the early stages of conflict.
   3. Three strategies to prevent the escalation of a conflict.
   4. Steps for conflict resolution; define, listen, reflect, and propose solutions.

The group leader can now develop strategies for each objective, allot and schedule time, and gather needed materials. For example:

Objective 1. Strategies: minilecture on different conflict behavior styles; short exercise and discussion about personal style, its impact and usual outcome; personal satisfaction with outcomes.

Objective 2. Strategies: minilecture and discussion.

Objective 3. Strategies: brainstorm prevention of escalation strategies; rank and discuss.

Objective 4. Strategies: presentation on conflict resolution steps; an exercise to demonstrate application to a personal conflict of members; discussion.

This schedule would also have time for the beginning, where introductions and collaborative goal setting could be done, and the ending, with a summary and evaluation. Times for the various components could also be adjusted.

● ● ● ● ●

Contained Learning and Tasks

Group leaders will need to be knowledgeable about the topics presented in the group to ensure that these do not require previous learning, and that these topics are not part of a need for sequential learning. In other words, the topics should be able to stand on their own in isolation. If sequential learning can be accomplished within the allotted time for the single session, it can be used. Leaders can reduce or eliminate considerable frustration for them and for group members if the idea of the self-contained topic for the session is followed.

It can also be crucial to not have out of group tasks to be completed by members. Since there is only one session, the leader does not usually give homework because there will not be an opportunity to fully explore or share the work in the group. Leaders should also resist asking members to do tasks/work prior to the session. While doing a task could be very rewarding and helpful, it would be the rare group where all members did the task prior to the session. If all members cannot participate because they did not do the homework assignment, that can negatively affect the group's process by causing that member or members to feel excluded or even produce shame, and that would make it difficult for the leader to promote inclusion and trust. In those circumstances, the potential benefits for the homework task would be lost or severely reduced. Homework is not recommended.

● ● ● ● ●

Understand and Accept the Process

Many group leaders would agree that some of the most important constraints are the lack of time and opportunity for the group process to unfold, such as experiencing movement through group stages; for members to engage in guided self-exploration in a safe environment; or for a deep and meaningful therapeutic relationship between the leader and members to develop. Group leaders can become very frustrated because they understand that these experiences can be valuable for group members' growth, development, and healing. The loss of potential is a major constraint.

It can be the loss of this potential that discourages some group leaders from capitalizing more fully on the time that is available. They can feel that it is futile to begin something rich and exciting that will be truncated or lost. A perspective that could be helpful is to view the single session as an opportunity to plant seeds of encouragement to participate in future group experiences that provide the time that is not available in this single session.

The group leader can understand that what can be done are some of the following:

- Introduce members to the possibilities for problem solving, for addressing their concerns and issues, and for learning more effective ways to relate, to communicate, or to cope.
- Reduce some of the ambiguity, uncertainty, apprehension, and anxiety about group process and procedures.
- Model the positive aspects of the therapeutic relationship and how this helps promote safety and trust.
- Demonstrate the benefits of verbalizing feelings, thoughts, and ideas and receive feedback for these.
- Produce some realistic hope for resolution, ability to cope, learning and growing, and the like.
- Identify unused or overlooked inner resources and strengths.
- Promote the value of connections and commonalities and thereby reduce feelings of alienation and isolation.

These possible outcomes are neither minor nor are they unimportant potentials for the single session, and group leaders who stay mindful of these can provide a very positive and rewarding experience even with the many constraints. What group members can take away from the single session can be encouraging and support members in engaging in additional group experiences, seeking out other learning opportunities, gaining a vision for greater self-efficacy, and so on.

● ● ● ● ●

Unplanned Single Sessions

Unplanned single sessions occur when one or more group members attend only one session of a group that is intended to have additional sessions. For example, the group is designed to have 12 sessions, but one or more members do not return after the first session. Although premature termination can occur at any time during the group's life span, and for various member reasons, this discussion is focused on the member who drops out after attending only one session. Some of the discussion and suggested strategies can also apply to premature terminations that occur after the first session.

The group leader has usually planned the group activities on the assumption that group members will attend all of the sessions and that there will be opportunities for the therapeutic relationship to develop over time, that some learning can be sequential and build on previous learning, and where the group's process can be a valuable resource to increase members' awareness and understanding. There could also be time for members to practice new behaviors, get ideas for more constructive ways to behave and to relate, become inspired and develop creative ideas for personal problem solving, and other positive outcomes. Significant and important changes take time to develop, be practiced, and become integrated, and these kinds of changes are the usual goals for the group. But, in order to effect change, group members need to attend and participate in their own growth, development, and healing. Members who prematurely terminate lose this opportunity.

While it can be the member who loses the most, the group leader can also be affected. Ofttimes a member who decides to stop attending the group does not provide notice of this intention. The leader is left adrift to try and analyze what happened to trigger the termination. For example, could it have been prevented, were there one or more precipitating incidents in the group that were not recognized or were ignored where a leader intervention would have been helpful? There are numerous possibilities for a group member's premature termination and the group leader has to consider that a leader or member action or inaction in the session played a role in the decision to not return to the group. This sort of analysis can help group leaders become more sensitive to the possibilities and potentials for premature terminations, devise strategies that may be preventive, and present sessions that will be constructive and helpful even when a member decides to leave the group. The latter is the central idea for this chapter; namely, to create and present each group session as self-contained even when the session is part of a series and members are expected to complete the full set of sessions.

● ● ● ● ●

Planning for Self-Contained Sessions

Once the leader accepts that there is the possibility that one or more members will attend a single session, or that others will prematurely terminate, the planning procedure becomes clearer, the possibilities and positive benefits for presenting sequential material are eliminated, and the focus is on what can be presented that is relevant and helpful, determining the most effective modalities for presenting, and choosing strategies and activities for the very limited goal(s) for each session. The group leader also accepts that the therapeutic relationship may not be developed with some group members, and that many helpful resources from the group may not be realized or used. The leader has to plan sessions for returning members as well as for members who may terminate during the course of the group. The basic structural planning factors include the following:

- Session introduction
- A major focus or goal for the session
- Strategies, activities, and techniques to be used
- Summary and closure

The *session introduction* need not be the same for each session, but could be a formalized, consistent procedure. Whereas the first session would begin with introductions and general information about group members, subsequent sessions could use this time for a meditation or a summary of the previous session, or some other activity to reorient members to the group. It could be helpful to have a planned introduction for each session.

Exercise 10.1

A recommended introductory activity for each session is to ask if anyone has something urgent and important to bring to the group; or after the first session, to ask if there is unfinished work from the previous session such as feelings or thoughts that were not expressed then but could be helpful to express now.

Each session should have *a major goal or focus* planned, even if the group leader has to abandon the prepared focus because the group has or wants to address something else that seems more important to them. Groups can have a sense of what they need, or what would be helpful, and the group leader has to be flexible enough to adjust rather than insisting that the group follow the planned agenda. A helpful approach after the first session could be to first ask the group what they think would be important to do in the session; or to propose a focus and ask for their input about its importance for that session. Group leaders should plan, but should not be insistent that the group follow that plan.

There are two group therapeutic factors that could be the focus for the first session—universality and hope. A focus on members' commonalities and similarities rather than their differences assists in the emergence of universality. It is essential that the group leader have an understanding that hope, especially realistic hope, is vital to members to encourage continued participation. This would also address one of the common member concerns about the experience, and how the group will help him or her. Planning to directly address this concern could provide some hope.

Strategies, activities, or techniques to be used can also be preplanned with the goal of providing members with some initial benefit(s) such as, new information, an awareness, encouragement, and support, coping skills, and so on. The theoretical perspective of the group leader and the needs of group members can guide the choice and selection of these. There are numerous ways to reach the same goal or address the session's focus. The type of group will also play a role in the selection, whether the group's purpose is educational, therapeutic, psychoeducational, or task-oriented. The important point is to think about what to do and how to do it before the session, and to gather any needed equipment and materials. Following are some examples for strategies and techniques categorized into task goals:

Dissemination of Information

- Media, such as video, DVD, Internet
- Lecture/discussion
- Readings
- Guest presenters

Building Awareness

- Brainstorming
- Art activities

- Writing activities
- Other creative activities
- Interactions among members

Skill Development

- Role play and behavioral rehearsal
- Demonstrations
- Practice with feedback

The final chapters of this book contain several activities that could be used for a single session.

Providing a *summary* of what transpired in the session and having a closure procedure could be beneficial for both the returning group members, and especially for those who will not return. A summary focuses their attention on the important elements of the session, can highlight progress, allows some moderation of intense feelings that may have been triggered, and suggests areas for further attention and exploration. A closure procedure can be an exercise, a ritual, or similar activity to mark the end of the group session and provide a transition to return to the world outside of the group. Having some ending procedure could benefit the member who may be prematurely terminating by giving that person closure for the group experience, reduce the likelihood of his or her carrying away important unfinished business that may have an impact, and can provide some possible material for reflection.

Managing Premature Termination

When a group member terminates after a single session, especially without notifying the leader in advance, the group leader faces several challenges. The first challenges are the ambiguity around the disappearance and the uncertainty as to its finality; that is, is this an absence for a session and the person will return, or is this absence a termination of the group experience? When a member does not give notice of his or her intention to terminate, it can arouse thoughts, feelings, and indecisiveness as to the best course of action to pursue.

The Leader

Let's explore the situation where the member attended the first session but without notice did not attend the second group session. The group leader only knows that this group member is absent after the group begins, and there could be numerous reasons. For example, the member could have been held up for some reason and will appear later, but even for a reasonable and rationale reason, the absence can produce lots of ambiguity and uncertainty for the group leader. Possible options at this point are to ask the group if anyone knows the person or his or her intent to attend, to wait and do or say nothing because of the possibility that the person is tardy, or to use outside sources to check on the person's intent to attend or not.

The first, and maybe most important concern is the leader's feelings at this point because these will influence the choice of intervention. Some leaders will have a rule or policy that group sessions begin and end at the designated time (this is recommended). Others will wait for a period of time to see if the person does appear. Still others may ask the group if they want to wait or to start the session. It could also be possible that some group leaders will leave the group to go and check on the absent member, or have someone check on him or her.

In addition to selecting an action, the leader also has to decide how to proceed using one of the following three options:

- Ignore the absence and continue with the plan for the session.
- Discuss the absence, its impact on the group, and members' feelings and reactions.
- Briefly mention the ambiguity and uncertainty, tell the group that the plan will be to wait to see if the absence is temporary or permanent, and then proceed with the planned session.

If the third option is chosen, the leader could also ask if there are any feelings or reactions to the absence or to the plan. Since this situation is the second group session, it may not be reassuring to group members if the absence is ignored (option 1), or if they are to make a decision as to what to do (option 2). The choice of action would depend on the group leader, and the composition of the group. The group that is still in stage 1 will have lots of concerns about safety and trust, and some members may have abandonment issues.

Group Members

Members can have many reactions and feelings, both expressed and unexpressed, and a group leader needs to be prepared for these to impact the group in direct and indirect ways, and to understand that these reactions can linger for several sessions. The unexpressed feelings that may even be unknown to the person can sometimes have the most significant impact. They can carry some important information about unresolved family of origin issues or other unfinished business from past relationships. This also includes the leader whose feelings about self-competency and other such countertransference can impact his or her functioning and how the group is to be managed and facilitated with this unexplained absence.

Members are likely to have many of the following thoughts, feelings, or reactions:

- They may wonder if they did or said something that was offensive or hurtful that caused the person to leave the group.
- They may be indifferent, rationalizing that they did not know the person and so feel nothing.
- They may question in what ways they were not good enough to keep the person from leaving the group.
- Members may rationalize or have fantasies about the absence or termination, such as the person has an emergency that was continuing.
- Members may be angry with the absent member for not attending and not giving notice of his or her intention to be absent.
- The absence may trigger abandonment issues that derive from members' family of origin and other past relationship experiences.
- There may be regrets that there was not an opportunity to connect with the absent person or to say goodbye.
- There may be fear that others will leave or that the leader will leave.
- There may be fear that the group is not safe.

Many of these feelings, especially those that are related to family of origin issues and past relationship concerns, may not be openly expressed but nevertheless, continue to exert an impact on the individual member, can influence the relationships with other members and with the leader, and may play a significant role in the quality of the individual's group participation.

These are feelings that are expressed and unexpressed or unknown to the person, and they can be a possible major influence on behavior that emerges or is displayed in the group in later sessions. For example, the reaction in the group of wondering or fearing that one did or said something that caused the person to terminate may be displayed as a tendency to self-blame, or of taking responsibility for others' actions, or of acting to soothe others' distress, or to work hard to prevent conflict from emerging in the group. The premature termination of a member could exacerbate already existing issues and concerns.

The Group's Functioning

There is also likely to be an impact from a termination on the group's functioning, such as there being more difficulty in developing trust and feelings of safety, and in forging a strong therapeutic alliance. Much of the impact is dependent on members' self-understanding of the personal associations they have about the termination, an awareness of how these associations may consciously or unconsciously affect their participation, and an opportunity to express these. The group leader's awareness of these possibilities allows him or her to intervene so as to reduce the negative impact, and to use the material in ways that will be beneficial for the individual and for the group.

Since the premature termination happened after the first session early in the life of the group, members may have conscious or unconscious concerns about the leader's competence and ability to hold the group together and keep members safe. This concern can be directly addressed by asking the group if this is a possible thought, and providing reassurance that the group will not disintegrate or be destroyed, with the caveat that members are in charge of their participation and, while you as the leader, are committed to the group, you also don't have the power to prevent other members from leaving. Even just openly speaking about the fear can be reassuring for some members. The leader's awareness of the potential impact and subsequent functioning of the group provides the opportunity for planning and prevention.

● ● ● ● ●

Sample Interventions

It may be helpful to provide some specific interventions such as the following: Group leaders can create or adapt interventions based on the group's characteristics and type. Each possible intervention will be discussed and suggested strategies provided.

- Discuss the termination; its ambiguity, uncertainty, and impact on the group and for individual members
- Emphasize the benefits of attendance and what the group feels like when a member is absent or tardy, with careful attention given to the positive effects of attendance.
- Focus on developing trust and safety throughout the life of the group.
- Highlight members' perceptions and feelings about the group and their roles.
- Provide opportunities for a group functioning checkup.

Discuss

It is important that the group leader not ignore, dismiss, or minimize the member's premature termination because to do so could send a message to the remaining group members that they too are not important or valued. On the other hand, you do not want or need to go to the other extreme and overly emphasize the importance of the termination. A middle ground approach would be to acknowledge the act, premature termination, and to hold a discussion that would allow group members to express their thoughts, feelings, reactions, and other possible associations. Members could find commonalties for these that may not have been verbalized except for the triggering premature action. The discussion need not be lengthy or time consuming, but if that is what happens, the leader then knows more about what members' issues and concerns are other than the identified ones that brought them to the group. Plans for sessions could then be adjusted to accommodate this new material.

Attendance

Another discussion that could be held is about members' expectations and hopes for their benefit from attending group sessions. This discussion could be an opportunity for the leader to emphasize the importance of attending all sessions, provide an overview of the course of the group, such as topics that will be covered, and use this material to engage in collaborative goal setting or revised goal setting. Individual members' goals, expectations, and hopes are combined into one or more group goals to meet the mission and purpose for the group. This discussion can also incorporate a discussion on what the group feels like when a member is absent or tardy. Sometimes members can feel that their presence isn't important but, although the group session is held, not only does the absent person miss out on information and interactions, but his or her contributions are missed. Think of how it must feel to miss a session, to realize that no one noticed or commented, or that your presence or absence is of no consequence to the group. This discussion can highlight the importance and unique contributions each member brings to the group.

Safety and Trust

Another topic that it can be helpful to bring to the surface is building trust and safety and how consistent attendance facilitates this, and the impact the premature termination may have on members, especially for those who have continuing issues around abandonment. Neither the group leader nor members who have this issue may be aware that it exists for them, but group leaders can anticipate that one or more group members may be affected. Trust and safety are concerns for all groups and a discussion about members' perceptions for these is helpful for all types of groups. Ask members what they need to feel safe in the group, and what promotes or retards their development of trust. This is where past experiences that produced feelings of rejection and betrayal may surface and can be related to or associated with this group experience.

Even though it may be a little early in the life of the group to highlight members' perceptions and feelings about the group, and their roles and place in the group, having a member prematurely terminate could arouse these concerns, and an open discussion could do much to clarify and to reassure members. The very act of talking about these topics can help reduce some of the anxiety members can have about the group experience in general, and that the premature termination could produce.

Following is an activity that I generally use later in the group's life, but could also be used after a member prematurely terminates.

Exercise 10.2 Image of the Group

Materials: Paper, a set of crayons or colored pencils for each group member, and a hard surface for drawing.

Procedure:

1. Ask the group to sit in silence, close their eyes, and focus their attention on the group as a whole.
2. Tell them to let an image of the group emerge, and as it emerges to not evaluate it or try to change it.
3. Allow 2 to 4 minutes for the imaging, and then instruct them to open their eyes and draw the image.
4. Reconvene in the circle and share the drawings.
5. Ask members what feelings they experienced as they allowed the image to emerge while drawing, and now as they are talking about the experience.
6. Summarize the themes from the drawings and feelings about the group.

Group Checkup

The final strategy presented is to do a group functioning checkup. Group members will have an opportunity to reflect and report on how well the group is functioning for them, and the leader can receive an indication of the impact of the premature termination on the group as a whole. This checkup can also be an opportunity to get members to express their perceptions and feelings to determine what is working well and what may need changing or additional attention. Following are two assessment instruments. The first is a rating scale, and the second is a semantic differential technique to assess attitudes.

Rating Scale

Directions: Reflect on your group experience to date and rate the items using the scale: 5—always or almost always; 4—often; 3—sometimes; 2—seldom; 1—never or almost never.

1. I understand the purpose and goal(s) for the group.   5 4 3 2 1
2. The group goals are consistent with my personal group
   goals.   5 4 3 2 1
3. The group feels safe to me.   5 4 3 2 1
4. I feel I can trust the group leader.   5 4 3 2 1
5. I feel that I can trust group members.   5 4 3 2 1
6. I think I will be helped by the group, or that my needs
   will be met.   5 4 3 2 1
7. The group is interesting and exciting.   5 4 3 2 1
8. The leader focuses on important material.   5 4 3 2 1
9. The extent and limits for confidentiality were fully
   explained to me.   5 4 3 2 1
10. I feel included in the group.   5 4 3 2 1

Scoring: You may either use a total score (10–50), or sum the ratings and derive the mean.

Semantic Differential

Directions: Check or circle the number between the set of adjectives that best fit your perception of the group.
EXAMPLE.

| Deadly | 1 2 3 4 <u>5</u> 6 7 8 9 | Lively |
| Up | 9 8 <u>7</u> 6 5 4 3 2 1 | Down |

The Group

Rich	9 8 7 6 5 4 3 2 1	Poor
Interesting	9 8 7 6 5 4 3 2 1	Dull
Boring	1 2 3 4 5 6 7 8 9	Exciting
Organized	9 8 7 6 5 4 3 2 1	Disorganized
Productive	9 8 7 6 5 4 3 2 1	Unproductive
Depressing	1 2 3 4 5 6 7 8 9	Cheerful
Ineffective	1 2 3 4 5 6 7 8 9	Effective
Inclusive	9 8 7 6 5 4 3 2 1	Exclusive

Good	9	8	7	6	5	4	3	2	1	Bad
Useful	9	8	7	6	5	4	3	2	1	Useless

Scoring: Compute the mean rating for each group member; the higher the mean, the more positive the perception. To derive the group's perception, compute the mean or means.

The focus for this chapter was on managing the group when a member leaves after the first session. Since premature termination can happen any time during the group's life span, the material is also appropriate for those situations.

11

• • • • •

Activities: Guidelines, Introductions, and Ice Breakers

The activities presented in this chapter are designed to be session contained because of the characteristics of open, single session, and self-help/mutual aid groups. Other types of leaderless groups are more likely to have a specific or cognitive focus, such as case review, where the emphasis is not so much on the group and its members' personal issues as would be the case for the other types of groups, and will have less need for activities such as those presented here. Presented are a brief overview of the literature, a list of some group situations that could be addressed with an activity even with an untrained group leader, basic considerations the leader should attend to prior to implementing an activity, and a description of the phases for implementing activities in the group.

• • • • •

Overview

Gladding (2003) writes about the use of creativity and spontaneity as a means of providing stimuli that may help then in accessing feelings and thoughts, especially those below the conscious level of awareness. Brown (2012) proposes that creative activities are helpful to assist group members in expressing difficult thoughts, feelings, and ideas, and as a guide to their discovery of their most important issues and concerns that may be in the nonconscious self. Bonhote, Romano-Egan, and Cornwell (1999) suggest that expressive communications "serve to enhance awareness of inauthentic attitudes, to facilitate acceptance of seemingly paradoxical aspects of human existence and to provide a deeper sense of life's meaningfulness" (pp. 613–614).

Expressive activities include drawing, collage, writing, imagery, dance and other movement exercises, poetry, music, literature, fairy tales, and other such stimuli that tap into one's senses. There is evidence that some expressive activities are helpful to individual members and to the group as a whole. Examples of some studies that support the use of these activities include the following:

- Writing (Pennebaker, 1997a, 1997b, 1999)
- Drawing (Ohnmeiss, Vanharanta, & Elkhorn, 1999)
- Fairy tales (Holton, 1995)
- Music (Williams et al., 2010)
- Dance (Langdon & Petracca, 2010)
- Imagery (Cameron, Booth, Schlatter, Ziginskas, & Harman, 2007)
- Poetry (Campo, 2003)

Uses for Activities

Activities are most useful when they are a compliment to the group and to its functioning. For example, *icebreakers* is one category of activity, and the purposes for these activities are to reduce some of the trepidation members can have about what to do by providing some structure; facilitate members' introductions to each other; elicit some important personal information that begins to promote universality among the members; and demonstrates ways to begin conversations with strangers outside of the group that members may find useful. Activities are less useful or can be detrimental to the group's progress when they are used excessively, as time fillers, or for other such reasons.

Constructive uses for activities include the following:

- As an energizer, for example when members are lethargic, exhibit deflated mood, or to promote interactions;
- As a focus to encourage self-reflection, emphasize positive aspects of the members, and to tap into unused inner resources;
- Provide an opportunity for every member to participate at the same time and keep the focus on the group and not on individual members which can reduce storytelling and monopolizing;
- To guide elaboration and exploration of personal issues and concerns;
- Facilitate expression of feelings by providing other means for expression, especially for expressing difficult feelings;

- Teach and practice communication and relating skills;
- Provide closure for the member and for the group so that there remains little or no unfinished business.

There are other reasons for using activities that are more suitable for therapy groups, especially closed and long term groups. The emphasis here will be on presenting activities being suitable for the challenging groups described in this book, and that the untrained group leader can facilitate. Careful attention is given to presenting activities that when used as described, are likely to be helpful, and have little or chance of being harmful.

Basic Considerations

There are five major considerations when using activities:

Group-Centered Rationale: The rationale for using any activity is to benefit the entire group. It is not helpful for other group members if an activity is focused on only one or two members. Group leaders are encouraged to select an activity to address a group concern such as a need to demonstrate constructive ways to handle conflicts, where all members can learn new ways of behaving and relating, increase awareness of self and of others, engage in self-exploration, and other such personal outcomes.

Time: Ensure that there is sufficient time to complete the activity, for all members to report, and to participate in some elaboration/exploration (Brown, 2012). These are explained more fully in the next session on phases. It is especially important to complete phases 3 (Producing) and 4 (Reporting). Do not try to carryover reporting until the next session as this can lessen the importance and intensity of members' experience with the activity.

Members' Abilities: It is important to select activities that are not too challenging for members' cognitive or physical abilities. For example, if some members have difficulties moving or walking around a room, an energizing or other movement exercise that requires them to do so would not be recommended as that would emphasize their differences, cause them to feel excluded if they could not participate, not fulfill the objective or goal for the activity, or produce feelings such as embarrassment, shame, anger or resentment. Stay mindful of group members' abilities to see, hear, read, understand directions, and physical capacities.

Environmental Concerns: There are also some environmental concerns that must receive attention, such as the following:

- The availability of hard surfaces for writing or drawing;
- Sufficient space for moving around without physical contact if physical movement is needed for the exercise;
- Privacy where outsiders cannot hear or see what is taking place in the group, and where the group is free from intrusions;
- Facilities for posting or writing directions, and other information for the group as a whole.

Materials: Group leaders should ensure that all materials are collected and available before introducing an exercise. There should be enough materials for each group member, especially items such as pens or pencils and paper. If you are using crayons or colored pencils or other drawing materials, two members can share these, but sharing among more than two members at one time can result in delays when members have to wait for a particular color, or their feelings about their product can be affected if they must choose a less desired color.

● ● ● ● ●

Fundamental Principles

This section presents the fundamental principles to guide the use of activities, general procedures for conducting the exercises, and a sample process for guiding members' personal exploration of their experiencing so as to facilitate their understanding of what emerges during the experience. The primary principles are as follows:

- The uniqueness of each member's personal experiencing.
- The group member provides his or her personal interpretation.
- Meanings lie within the individual.
- Products can provide clues for what is needed by that person.
- Reduction of defensiveness.
- Promote and increase acceptance of what emerges for the person.
- The emergence of developmental and existential issues.
- Experiencing does not end with completion of the activity.
- Intense emotions can be triggered.

Each member's personal experience is unique and can be an interaction of many factors such as past experiences, family of origin factors, personality, current physical and emotional states, and so on. Thus, each group member's experiencing will be unique and personally relevant for him or her, to be interpreted by that person.

The leader does not interpret for group members, either the product or the associations the member may have, nor does the leader allow other members to interpret for each other. Other members may report on their experiencing, or the feelings and thoughts that emerge as they listen to each other, but it should be clear that these are not interpretations for others' experiencing.

The meanings for what emerges lie within that person, but do tend to reflect the person's current inner world. Even past experiences that can be the product of an activity or an association are perceived from that member's current perspective.

The products or outcomes provide clues for the person's current wishes, desires, and needs, and the like. The cues and their messages and meaning carry personal implications that are lurking below the person's conscious awareness or even are emerging from the nonconscious. These cues, messages, meaning, and any other associations are best analyzed and interpreted by that person.

Members tend to be less defensive when they produce the meanings for the activity or the product when they make their own personal interpretations versus when the group leader or other members provide interpretations. They can be more likely to explore pathways of understanding and insight that become open because their energy is used to understand instead of resisting the material that emerges, or others' interpretations.

When the group member provides meaning for his or her products, that person can be more accepting of what emerges during the activity as the threat or danger to the self from the material is managed better when the person in question is in control.

Developmental and existential issues can be tapped with some activities and because these are issues and concerns that continue to reemerge throughout life, the activity provides an opportunity for understanding to emerge. When these issues do emerge, the leader can help members to become aware that this continuation is expected, that answers derived are only for the current time and may not apply at other times, and to gain a better understanding of the impact these can and do have on their functioning. Activities can activate these issues, bring them to the member's conscious awareness, provide a means to express these, and to become aware that there may be others in the group who are struggling with the same or similar issues and concerns.

Learning, understanding, and insight can continue after the activity and the session are completed. Group members can continue to reflect on what was experienced, and additional learning, understanding, and even repressed memories can emerge after the activity is completed, and between group sessions. The continued processing of the experience can contribute to the member's growth, development, and healing.

While the activities presented in this book should not evoke extreme emotions, the group leader must be mentally and emotionally prepared to cope with members' intense, and sometimes unexpected, emotions that can emerge during an activity. The group leader has to ensure that the members do not become mired or overwhelmed with the emotional intensity, and that they are managing their emotions well when they leave the session.

Ethical principles provide standards for the use of expressive exercises, with education and training required in the use of some. However, the activities presented in this book were chosen so that specialized training is not required, and untrained group leaders can use them. It is suggested that it would be helpful for leaders to get some training, such as attending workshops, conference institutes, and other means of training.

● ● ● ● ●

Common Member Reactions and Their Rationales

Reasons vary within and among group members: Most often, members will have different reasons and sources for their reactions. For example, some could be experiencing transference, some are projecting, some fear destruction of the self, and others could be so fearful of what could emerge that they shut down. The group leader may not know or be aware of all of the individual reasons, and each may need a different intervention, but the entire group is still impacted and reacting.

Reactions can reflect resistance, confusion, fear, or uncertainty: Resistance to what can emerge about one self; confusion about what is being felt but not understanding one's feelings; confusion about the dissonance in the group and its sources; fear of destruction or abandonment of the self; and uncertainty with all of its accompanying terror.

● ● ● ● ●

Basic Conditions

There are several basic group conditions that guide the use of activities when sufficient safety and trust have been developed: there are rules and guidelines for participation and for giving and receiving feedback. It is critical to develop sufficient safety and trust before conducting most of the described activities. The only exceptions may be when an activity is used to facilitate introduction of members where the activity is non-threatening, and does not call for disclosure of sensitive personal material; or using an activity to just play and have fun. Safety and trust will facilitate self-disclosure by members, and the level to which they are willing to reveal the real self.

Group leaders will usually have collaboratively established rules and guidelines for participation, will review these with members to get their commitment, and members will generally know what is expected for communication, disclosure, and providing feedback to each other. It is recommended that members be put in charge of their disclosure to decide when and how much to disclose, and that neither the leader nor other members push for a deeper level of disclosure. It is also helpful if members know that courtesy and civility are expected in relating and communicating among each other, but not to the extent where nothing significant is communicated. Labeling, calling names, being disrespectful, and those sorts of activities are to be prohibited and blocked.

Relationships are enhanced when the members can be open and direct with each other in their relationships, but that also carries the responsibility of being tolerant, respectful, and mindful when giving and receiving feedback. It is helpful for the group leader to teach group members constructive ways to provide feedback, and to help members learn how to receive and accept feedback. These competencies will facilitate personal learning from the creative activities.

There are times when the group needs assistance to express their thoughts, ideas, and feelings in appropriate ways. One of the reasons that some difficult situations or group dilemmas occur is that members are reluctant to express negative feelings because they fear the fantasized outcomes to be destructive, either to them, to the leader, or to the group. The leader's expertise, and use of creative activities can facilitate expression and demonstrate how to do so appropriately. Most of all, members can learn that feedback need not be negative or destructive.

Group members can also learn problem solving through participation in creative activities, especially when things are complex, ambiguous, and uncertain as these occur in the group setting. Demonstrating that there are alternative perspectives, different means to approach a problem or dilemma, and even just the use of creativity can suggest to members that problems need not be overwhelming and frustrating to the point where nothing constructive is accomplished.

Other Assumptions

- The stage of the group is influential, especially when choosing an activity.
- The therapeutic relationship with the leader is also a critical component; the extent of development for the relationship.
- The level of trust and safety established among group members and with the leader.

Phases

In order to derive the maximum benefit from activities, five phases of development can be implemented; creating, planning, producing, reporting, and elaboration/expanding. The first phase is called *creating* to emphasize the need to find appropriate activities and to tailor any such exercise or activity to fit a particular group, or to encourage the group leader to create an exercise or activity. Either way, the group leader has to think about the group and how the activity will be developed or adjusted. Finding activities is not difficult; there are numerous books available, many of which can be found on the Internet.

The *planning* phase includes specifying the goals and objectives, estimating time needed, reviewing the space needs, and securing needed materials.

1. A goal and some objectives are helpful to focus the exercise on essential needs for the group. Review the list of possible goals and objectives presented at the beginning of this chapter to determine if one of these is appropriate for your group, or develop one that is more suitable for your needs. Limit the goal and objective to one each, because trying to accomplish more can lead to confusion about the intent and purpose for the exercise or activity, or produce the inability to successfully attain any of them.
2. Estimate the time needed to complete all aspects of the activity from introduction to all members having an opportunity for elaboration/expanding. The activity is more helpful and powerful when all aspects can be completed in the session. The number of members in the group is a large determiner of the time that will be needed. One possible guide is to allow at least one or more minutes per member for reporting, and 3 to 5 minutes per member for elaboration/expansion.

3. Review the space needs for the exercise. Are hard surfaces available for writing or drawing? Is there a board or easel for posting directions? Is there sufficient space for member to move around if movement is a part of the exercise? How can privacy be ensured from external sources such as people passing by and looking in a window?
4. Collect all materials needed. Construct a list of materials and the number needed for each. Using a list can help ensure that everything needed will be readily available and in sufficient numbers.

The *producing phase* implements the activity in the group. Provide an introduction that fully describes the purpose and intent of the exercise, the procedure and directions for completion, the time given for each step, answer questions and provide clarification, and most importantly, ask members if they can or will participate. It is generally helpful to have posted the directions, or to now reveal the directions that were written on a large sheet of newsprint, or on a chalk or smart board, or projected from a slice. After the introduction, distribute the materials, and instruct members to begin. Repeat the time given for completing the activity, such as, "You have 10 minutes to complete the drawing." Also notify group members when there are 2 to 3 minutes left for completion.

After completing the products or activity, reconvene the group in a circle for the *reporting phase*. This is the time when each group member describes the product, such as a drawing, without questions or telling stories. Some discussion can take place, but most of that should be saved for the *elaboration/explanation phase* in the interest of time. It is essential that every group member has an opportunity to present his or her product and to say a few words about it. Leaders should restrict their comments to a very few during this phase, and not ask questions that call for an extensive answer. The leader can also ask members to report on feelings experienced while completing the exercise or while reporting on it to the group.

The final phase can be the *elaboration/exploration phase* if there is sufficient time. Although group leaders plan so that there is time for all phases, there are occasions where members take longer than intended to complete the product or for the reporting. This can be especially true when the group has many members. It is recommended that the *production* and *reporting phases* not be truncated, and that the final phase be implemented if there is time. If there is some time, but not enough for each member to engage in exploration/elaboration, the group leader can ask for volunteers, such as asking members who wants to talk about their product, associations that emerged, and other thoughts and feelings they have. Depending on the amount of time remaining, the leader can explore feelings members have about the exercise, their personal involvement with it, and how helpful it was for them.

The remainder of this section presents activities and exercises than can be used in some of the challenging groups. These should be sparingly used, and not be the focus for every session. The activities are categorized as:

- Ice breakers and introductions designed for new members or the new group, found in the remainder of this chapter;
- Self-reflecting and expressing emotions—chapter 12;
- Communication skills and closure—chapter 13.

● ● ● ● ●

Ice Breakers and Introductions

The main consideration in selecting ice breaker and introductory activities is that the exercise should involve the entire group in presenting. While it can be helpful to break the group into dyads or triads for exercises, especially when time is at a premium that would mean that all members do not get to hear from each other. For example, a common exercise is to break the group into dyads and have each duo interview each other with a list of set items, and then introduce each other to the group. However, during the interview the dyads have an opportunity to do more than just answer the item that will be used in the introduction, to express some feelings, and to provide other information. Hence, that duo makes connections that other group members do not, and could at some point, produce a subgroup or clique. The approach recommended here is that exercises focus on members presenting themselves to the group, even when they may work alone first. The other recommendation is that any activity chosen be short as the objective is to allow members to reduce some of the ambiguity and uncertainty about the group experience as well as to make connections with each other. All activities presented here are designed for groups where all members are present at the first session. Activities for integrating and introducing new members into open groups are presented in the section on those groups.

Exercise: 11.1 Who Am I?

Materials: ATC cards or 2½" × 3½" cardstock and a set of crayons, felt markers, or colored pencils for each member; and a suitable surface for drawing

Procedure:

1. The group leader should prepare a sample card in advance that illustrates how symbols can be used, but not try to present the leader's personal characteristics. For example, a house could be drawn to illustrate the value of family, a flower for the importance of creativity, a heart to illustrate caring and concern, and so on.

2. Introduce the exercise by explaining that each member is asked to select some symbols to illustrate some of their characteristics, interests, and values that they want other members to know about them. Use the materials to draw the symbols. It is important to tell group members that artistic ability is not a requisite, and that either representative symbols or abstractions, or even splashes of color can be used as illustrations.

3. Allow enough time for members to draw, but try to keep it to about 10 minutes.

4. Ask group members to share their cards with the group. Be sure to have all members share their cards before exploring any symbols and the like.

5. Explore the activity by asking members:
   - What was it like to think of symbols and to draw them?
   - Did anyone decide to not illustrate something about themselves that popped up as they thought about the activity? (Do not ask what it was.)
   - What feelings were aroused as they thought about what to present about themselves?
   - What feelings were aroused as they presented their cards? Listened to others' presentations?

Exercise 11.2 A Valued Object

Materials: None

Procedure:

1. Introduce the exercise by telling members to think of a valued material object they possess. Many people will want to tell about a valued relationship, but ask them to focus on an object.

2. Ask each member to describe their object, and say a few words about its value to him or her.

3. After each member has shared his or her object, explore the experience:
   - What feelings emerged as you thought about your object?
   - Did you have more than one object that came to mind?
   - Was it difficult or easy to think of an object?
   - What feelings emerged as you presented about your object? Listened to others present about their objects?

Exercise 11.3 Squares

Materials: A large sheet of newsprint (16" × 20" or larger) with lines drawn to form six large squares where each square has the following headings: Achievements, a Value, Leisure Activity, Current Feelings, a Current Concern, and a Favorite Song; and a set of felt markers of sufficient number so that each group member can have a different color.

Procedure:

1. Post the newsprint and ask group members to select one felt marker.
2. Tell them to write one item in each square.
3. Once the squares are filled, review these with the group. Point out similarities among the entries.
4. Discuss what feelings emerged as they completed the exercise, and as they reviewed the lists.

Exercise 11.4 Tags

Materials: A name tag for each group member, and either small stickers of animals, birds, etc. or felt markers in a variety of colors for drawing and writing.

Procedure:

1. Ask group members to pick up a name tag and write their name on it.
2. Select either a sticker that represents something about them, or use the felt markers to draw a symbol for the same.
3. Ask each member to give their name, the name or nickname by which they want to be addressed in the group, and to describe their symbol.
4. Hold a discussion about the feelings that emerged as they completed each part of the exercise.

Exercise 11.5 My Public Self

Materials: ATC cards or cardstock cut into 2½" × 3½" pieces—one for each group member, a selection of magazines and catalogues from which to cut images, scissors, glue or glue sticks, and a set of felt markers. Provide a suitable surface for drawing.

Procedure:

1. Introduce the exercise by telling members that most people have several layers of the self, and that one layer is the public layer, the self that is presented to and seen by others. Distribute the materials and ask them to make a collage of images or of drawings that illustrates their public self. Allow 10 to 15 minutes for construction.

2. Reconvene the group in a circle and ask members to share their cards.

3. Hold a discussion about how easy or hard it was to select, find, or draw images for the self, did they censor or evaluate the images before pasting, the feelings that emerged as they created the card, feelings that emerged during others' reports, and sharing their own cards.

12

Activities:
Self-Reflection and
Expressing Emotions

• • • • •

Self-Reflection Activities

This next set of exercises is designed to encourage self-reflection, to increase group members' awareness, especially about positive aspects of self. It seems relatively easy for some people to highlight their perceived flaws, mistakes, and the like, but to also shy away from recognizing their positive resources and actions. There can also be others who inflate their positive attributes and minimize or fail to recognize their behaviors, attitudes, and the like that have a negative impact on others and on their relationships. Participating in the kind of self-reflection produced by these exercises can present opportunities for members to gain a more balanced self-perception.

Exercise 12.1 Evaluating Wellness

Goals: Increase awareness of wellness and the issues that surround it. Set personal priorities for wellness.

Materials: Paper and pencil for each participant, a list of the following areas for each participant or the list posted on newsprint or on a chalk/whiteboard. The leader should either write each of the categories on a separate sheet of newsprint, or if using a board, on separate boards to list members' responses.

Example: Wellness Quality: Means of Evaluation

Wellness Categories

Physical	Inspirational/Spiritual	Relational
Zest/vitality	Cognitive/thinking	Creative/ideas
Emotional	Self-accepting	Lifestyle habits

Procedure:

1. Introduce the exercise by telling group members that each of the listed items is an aspect of wellness. The task is for them to create a list of wellness qualities for each of the areas, and describe how each can be evaluated. For example, a wellness quality for Physical wellness could include a body weight within medical guidelines for height and body frame. This could be evaluated by weighing oneself. Another example could be having meaning and purpose for one's life as a wellness quality for Inspirational/Spiritual. This could be evaluated by the level of personal satisfaction with this quality.

2. Use the newsprint or chalk/whiteboard to list members' ideas, and remind them that you want a response from every member.

3. Lead a discussion about the qualities for each category and focus on members' feelings about the items, their personal satisfaction with their wellness for the quality, what could or should be changed to gain greater satisfaction, and the like.

Note: This exercise could be completed over several sessions so as to give ample time for discussion of each quality, evaluate it, and to add additional ones.

Exercise: 12.2 Physical Self

Note: This is one of six possible exercises about the self, 12.2 to 12.7: Physical, Emotional, Inspirational/Spiritual, Mental, and Relational. Each can be used alone, or as a part of a series with the other five exercises.

Materials: A list of the behaviors and attitudes relative to physical health, pencils or pens, paper for each participant.

Procedure:

1. Introduce the exercise by telling participants that the physical self is an important component for their general overall health and well-being. The exercise is intended to focus on those aspects of the physical self that are satisfactory, those that could be better and are under the person's control, and to develop an action plan to strengthen all aspects of one's physical self.

2. Distribute the materials, and ask them to rate each item.

3. Ask group members to share the top two or three with the highest ratings, and two or three that could use some attention or work. Be sure to note commonalties among the ratings for items.

4. A discussion about each item and the levels of satisfaction could be held at this point if there is sufficient time.

5. After the sharing is complete, ask members to write some goals they feel could be helpful, what would be an indicator that the goal had been reached or that significant progress is being made to achieve the goal, and a date when they intend to implement the first step toward the goal.

6. Ask the members to share one or more goals in the group. Be sure to allow enough time so that every member gets to talk about at least one of his or her goals, outcome measures, and intended beginning date.

● ● ● ● ●

Physical Self-Rating Scale

Directions: Rate the extent to which you are satisfied with each of the following items, using the scale below:

5—extremely well satisfied; 4—very well satisfied; 3—satisfied;
2—dissatisfied; 1—extremely or very dissatisfied

1. My diet habits.	5 4 3 2 1
2. The level of energy I have most days.	5 4 3 2 1
3. The extent to which I exercise.	5 4 3 2 1
4. Caffeine intake.	5 4 3 2 1
5. Bodily tension.	5 4 3 2 1
6. Sleep patterns.	5 4 3 2 1
7. Body image.	5 4 3 2 1
8. Physical pain.	5 4 3 2 1
9. Smoking habits.	5 4 3 2 1
10. Current weight	5 4 3 2 1
11. Alcohol use.	5 4 3 2 1
12. Sexual satisfaction.	5 4 3 2 1
13. Stamina.	5 4 3 2 1
14. Strength.	5 4 3 2 1

Goals

Exercises 12.3–12.7

The same materials and procedure are used for exercises 12.3 to 12.7. What follows are the rating scales for those exercises.

Exercise 12.3 Emotional Self-Rating Scale

Leader Directions: Ask members to first rate each item, and then rate their satisfaction with the rating/item.

Directions: Rate the extent to which you experience each of the following items using the scale.

5—frequently or almost always; 4—very often; 3—often;
2—seldom; 1—never or almost never

1. I feel sad or depressed.	5 4 3 2 1
2. I tend to be anxious.	5 4 3 2 1
3. I am unhappy.	5 4 3 2 1
4. I worry a lot, even over minor things.	5 4 3 2 1
5. I can catch others' feelings.	5 4 3 2 1
6. I can easily express positive feelings.	5 4 3 2 1
7. I can easily express negative feelings.	5 4 3 2 1
8. It is easy for me to openly express my anger.	5 4 3 2 1
9. It is easy for me to openly express love and appreciation.	5 4 3 2 1
10. I tend to express thoughts or thoughts about my feelings instead of the feelings.	5 4 3 2 1

Exercise 12.4 Inspirational Self-Rating Scale

Directions: Rate your level of satisfaction with each of the following:

5—extremely satisfied; 4—very satisfied; 3—satisfied;
2—dissatisfied; 1—very dissatisfied

1. My hope for the future.	5 4 3 2 1
2. The meaning and purpose for my life.	5 4 3 2 1
3. My values and how I live up to them.	5 4 3 2 1
4. My optimism and positive outlook on life.	5 4 3 2 1
5. I lead by example.	5 4 3 2 1
6. I feel at peace with myself and where I am in life.	5 4 3 2 1
7. I have direction for my life.	5 4 3 2 1
8. I feel connected to others and to the universe.	5 4 3 2 1
9. I gain inspiration from a variety of sources.	5 4 3 2 1
10. My religion/spirituality is a source of comfort for me.	5 4 3 2 1

Exercise 12.5 Cognitive/Mental Self-Rating Scale

Directions: Rate the extent of your personal satisfaction with each of the following:

5—extremely satisfied; 4—very satisfied; 3—satisfied;
2—dissatisfied; 1—very dissatisfied

1. My mental alertness.   5 4 3 2 1
2. Short-term memory.   5 4 3 2 1
3. Long-term memory.   5 4 3 2 1
4. Ability to think logically and rationally.   5 4 3 2 1
5. My curiosity and imagination.   5 4 3 2 1
6. Ability to recall facts, events, and the like.   5 4 3 2 1
7. The extent to which I can generate new ideas.   5 4 3 2 1
8. Ability to think through problems and generate solutions. 5 4 3 2 1
9. My insight and awareness about myself and others.   5 4 3 2 1
10. My intellectual sharpness and acuity.   5 4 3 2 1

Exercise 12.6 Relational Self-Rating Scale

Directions: Rate your level of satisfaction with each of the following items:

5—extremely satisfied; 4—very satisfied; 3—satisfied;
2—dissatisfied; 1—very dissatisfied

1. The quality and number of my friendships.   5 4 3 2 1
2. My ability to form and maintain intimate relationships.   5 4 3 2 1
3. My ability to handle conflict in a constructive manner.   5 4 3 2 1
4. I understand and use social graces and social convention.   5 4 3 2 1
5. My ability to say no and stick to it.   5 4 3 2 1
6. I can initiate social contact, and sustain conversations.   5 4 3 2 1
7. My family of origin relationships overall.   5 4 3 2 1
8. My current family relationships (if different from family of origin).   5 4 3 2 1
9. Helpfulness and responsiveness to others.   5 4 3 2 1
10. My social life.   5 4 3 2 1

Exercise 12. 7 Zest and Vitality

Goal: Identify personal life strengths and weaknesses that relate to zest and vitality.

Directions: Advance preparation. Develop definitions for the following, and write them on newsprint that can be posted where everyone can see.

Materials: A copy of the following list for all group members, and a pen or pencil for writing.

Nutritional practices for physical vitality;
Physical fitness, the role of exercise, medication, physical health;
Encouragement and support from family and other important people in your life;
Managing and coping with changes—either planned or unplanned;
Meaningful and satisfying work;
Growth and stimulation, such as creativity and inspiration;
An optimistic and realistic attitude;
Satisfying and enduring relationships;
Appropriate sense of humor;
Support network of family and friends;
Letting go of negatives, such as being able to forgive.

Procedure:

1. Introduce the exercise by noting that there are many aspects to one's life and that many people have unrecognized and unused personal resources that could contribute to making their lives more meaningful and enjoyable. Note that the list provided has only some of these aspects.

2. Ask members to give examples for each item on the list, and write these beside or under that item on the newsprint.

3. Once the examples are completed, ask members to give each item a rating that describes their competence for the item. 5—extremely competent; 4—very competent; 3—competent sometimes; 2—not competent much of the time; 1—unable to maintain competency

4. Ask members to then share their top two or three competencies (ratings of 4 and 5), and their lowest three competencies (ratings of 1 and 2)

5. The final step is to ask them to identify one or two steps they could take to increase their competencies for the lowest rated items, and to rate their commitment on a scale of 1 (low) to 5 (highly committed) to implement the steps.

Exercise 12. 8 Self-Nurturing

Goals: To help members identify ways that they can nurture and energize themselves.

Materials: Drawing paper, pencils, and a set of crayons, felt markers, or colored pencils for each participant. Or, collage—one or two ATC cards (2½" × 3½"), magazines for cutting images and symbols, or these can be precut by the leader; stickers, glue, and drawing implements for each participant. The following items printed on newsprint and posted where group members can easily see them. A surface for drawing or constructing the collage.

Posted on newsprint:
Draw or find a symbol to represent
   The life experiences that fill your heart
   Something that nourishes your self-concept
   Something that inspires and contributes to your productivity
   An experience that restores or revitalizes you
   Unanticipated pleasure
   Life savors

Procedure:

1. Introduce the exercise and distribute the materials.

2. Tell group members that they can nurture themselves in many ways. While others provide nurturing and comfort, it can also be important for them to use some self-care coping strategies.

3. Call attention to the posted items as examples of some self-nurturing resources, and ask that they draw or find the symbols or items to represent these.

4. Give them the time frame for drawing or constructing the collage, such as 20 minutes. Remind them of the time remaining to complete the projects when there are about 2 to 3 minutes remaining.

5. Convene the group and ask members to share their products.

6. Expand and explore the activity by asking them to respond to the following questions:
   What feelings emerged as you thought about the various self-nurturing resources?
   What feelings did you have during construction?
   What feelings emerged as you shared your project, and listened to others' sharing?
   How would you summarize your thoughts, feelings, and ideas about your nurturing and energizing sources after completing the activity?
   Did any new awareness emerge for you? If so, what can you do about the awareness?

Exercise 12.9 Pleasurable Activities

Goals: To assist members in identifying pleasurable activities that can increase or produce a positive mood, decrease stress, and enhance a sense of well-being.

Materials: A sheet of paper and writing instrument for each group member.

Procedure:

1. Distribute the materials and ask members to rate their current mood at this moment on a scale of 1—very sad or depressed to 10—joyful.

2. Introduce the exercise by stating the goal and telling members that sometimes in the press of everyday life we can forget to focus on the positive aspects, and even fail to do things that bring us pleasure.

3. Ask members to list 10 or more activities that bring them pleasure. These activities can be minor such as eating ice cream, or major such as attending an event (sporting, performance, music, party, etc.) The activities that they list should be those that they can initiate and are not solely dependent on others, although others may be involved. Allow about 10 to 15 minutes to create the lists.

4. Remind members when there are a couple of minutes remaining to finish the list, call time, and convene in the circle to share the lists.

5. After sharing their lists, ask them to note beside each the last time they engaged in the activity (e.g., day, week, month, year).

6. Ask members to report on what emerged for them as they constructed their lists, reported, and recalled the last time they engaged in the activity. Try to focus on the feelings.

7. Explore what barriers there are that keep them from engaging in any or all of the activities that bring them pleasure, and what they can do to have more of these.

8. The final step is to have members rate their current mood after completing the exercise, and to note the contrast (if any) with the mood as they began the exercise.

● ● ● ● ●

Expressing Emotions

It can be very helpful to the group's and individual's progress to facilitate their expression of feelings, and this next set of activities focuses on helping members identify and express these, whether positive or negative. Some members will find it relatively easy to express their thoughts as feelings; to express thoughts about feelings, identify sensations as feelings, but will not find it easy to express feelings, especially in the here and now.

It is important that group members learn to distinguish between thoughts and feelings, become aware of what they are feeling at all times, learn to openly and directly express feelings when appropriate and in appropriate ways, learn enough feeling words to be more precise when identifying their feelings, increase awareness and ability to identify what about the person or event arouses these feelings, and realize when triggered feelings are a playback of old parental messages that can produce guilt or shame.

Growth, development, healing, and interpersonal relationships can be enhanced in the group when members will verbally express important feelings. This is one way that they can become more in-tune with what others are feeling but may be unable to effectively express, and become more sensitive to nuances and subtleties of feelings.

Group members may want to also increase their awareness of when they are suppressing or repressing important feelings. Some indices of suppression and repression of important feelings in the group are when they experience any of the following: bored, tired, numb, blank or nothing, rebellious and defiant, want to attack another person or the leader, resigned, or turned off. In addition to suppression and repression, they can rationalize not expressing their feelings with thoughts like the following:

- I don't want to offend.
- The group won't like me, I'll be rejected.
- The leader will disapprove or think less of me.
- The other person may feel rejected.
- If I say what I really think, it may provoke conflict.

While the member who has any of the previous thoughts may think that they are being considerate of others, what they are really doing is protecting themselves against being aware of their personal issues, concern or feelings (e.g., guilt and shame). The fear of being rejected is more apparent but it is still disguised because it is really a fantasy or a projection.

The fear of provoking conflict can also be a projection. Some degree of conflict is already present in the group and what can be happening when members do not express their thoughts and feelings will tend to keep conflict hidden instead of allowing it to emerge before it intensifies. If allowed to emerge, conflict has the potential to be constructively resolved and to strengthen relationships.

Thinking about a feeling removes the person from fully expressing a feeling, promotes intellectualization, reduces the intensity associated with the feeling, and allows the person to keep important information submerged. An example of a thought that is not a feeling can be seen in the statement, "That must be very hard for you." An example of a thought about a feeling is seen in the statement, "I feel that I'm in a difficult situation." Expressing a sensation instead of a feeling is seen in the statement, "I'm uncomfortable."

Identifying feelings begins with a sensation that the person can name or label. The sensation can be mild or intense, and is experienced, embraced, pushed aside or, rejected. When pushed aside or rejected, it can become a thought about a feeling that then lessens its potential threat. Members could benefit from becoming more aware of when they express thoughts instead of feelings. Some common comments members can make that illustrate use of thoughts instead of feelings include:

"It was interesting."
"I got a lot out of it."
"The leader was (good, or not good)"
"I just wanted it to end."
"It was a good experience."
"My group never jelled."

Some feelings could be inferred from the statements, but thoughts were expressed, not feelings.

Following are some exercises to promote expression of feelings.

Exercise 12.10 Interruptions

Materials: One or more sheets of paper for each participant, and a pen or pencil for writing.

Procedure:

1. The leader can prepare a poster in advance with the following on it, or can write the terms on a chalk or blackboard.
   a. Visual;
   b. Auditory;
   c. Taste;
   d. Tactile or Feeling;
   e. Smell

2. Introduce the exercise by telling group members that they can control the intensity of distressing feelings with an interruption when these feelings emerge. The interruption is one of the images they will develop by participating in the exercise. For example, if they find that they are becoming angry, they can image or think of one of the interruptions that are listed in the exercise.

3. Use the poster or list of terms and give your examples for each, such as
    a. Visual—kittens playing;
    b. Auditory—cool jazz tunes;
    c. Taste—coffee in the morning;
    d. Tactile—silk scarf on neck;
    e. Smell—fresh popcorn popping
4. Ask group members to identify one or more examples for each term.
5. Ask members to share their answers in the group. If there are multiple group sessions, ask members to try the interruptions and to bring what happened back to the group.

Exercise 12.11 Colors and Feelings

Materials: The leader should prepare the following in advance. Cut 1" × 2" strips of 8 to 15 different colors of paper. Cut one or more strips of the same color for each group member; for example, if there are eight members in the group you would cut 16+ strips of each color; a sheet of paper for each member, glue sticks, and pens for writing.

Procedure:

1. Distribute the materials and introduce the exercise by asking members to list the major feelings they have experienced in the last month, select a color for each feeling, and glue the strip of colored paper for the feeling beside the name of it on the list. Tell members to be sure to list graduations of feelings, not just intense ones. For example, they list irritation as well as anger.
2. Give time for them to complete their lists and gluing.
3. Ask them to either turn the sheet of paper over, or if there is room, to write at the bottom of the page. They are asked to write what thoughts, feelings, and ideas they became aware of as they completed the task, and now as they are reviewing the experience.
4. Ask members to share their feelings list and colors, or what they wrote.
5. Explore the exercise by asking them to respond to the following:
    Which feelings were easy to list and find a color for?
    Which feelings were difficult to list and find a color for?
    Were they limited by the choices of colors?
    What did they become aware of as they completed the task, shared their products, and now as they reflect on the exercise?

Exercise 12.12 Validating and Managing Feelings

Materials: Several sheets of paper for each member, and a pen or pencil for writing. Prepare a list of possible strategies on newsprint, and post when ready for step 3.

Possible Strategies:
> Use logical and rational self-statements (e.g., I'm not competent in all things, but I am competent in some things).
> Block the feeling off and examine it later.
> Use emotional insulation (Imagine something between you and the other person that screens out their words or actions that are distressing for you. You can hear what they are saying, but you aren't taking it in. You can imagine a wall, steel door, force field, curtain, shade, or anything similar).

Procedure:

1. Introduce the exercise by telling group members that this is a process that can help with managing intense feelings such as anger, shame, guilt, and fear.

2. Ask members to write the answers to the following as you guide them through the process.
   Containing and Managing Your Feelings:
   a. Identify, name, or label a distressing feeling you've experienced, and the action that triggered the feeling. Give the distressing feeling a rating of 0—no distress to 10—considerable distress.
   b. Embedded in the feeling is a self-statement or thought about your essential self. Identify the statement about your essential self that the action triggered (The leader reads the following list slowly).
   I'm inadequate.
   I'm incompetent.
   I'm shameful.
   I will be abandoned.
   I will be destroyed.
   I cannot take care of myself.
   I am powerless.
   I am hopeless.
   I am helpless.
   c. Associate the self-statement, or fear, with previous situations, such as the following:
   Old parental messages about your worth and value that seem to be dismissive of you, or invalidating.
   Sibling relationships such as feeling that you were not treated as fairly as your sibling(s).
   Other past relationships that were not satisfying.
   d. Reflect on the possibility that your current feeling is more associated with one of the parental, sibling, or other relationships than

it is with the person or action at the current time, and write your answer (e.g., yes, no, could be).

   e. Review the distressing feeling you identified at the beginning, and give it a distress rating now (0–10).

3. Post the possible strategies and ask members to review them and see if any of them fit. Hold a discussion so that all group members get an opportunity to share. Tell them that they can imagine their emotional insulation at any time even in the middle of a conversation.

4. Review the following as actions to avoid (Note: the leader can also prepare a poster of these suggestions):

Blame someone for "making" you feel as you do (e.g., "You make me so mad").

Expect the other person to change, soothe, or reassure you because you want them to.

Intensify negative feelings with negative self-statements.

Try to arouse guilt, shame, nurturing feelings in the other person.

Expect empathy or understanding from the other person, but appreciate these when they do appear.

Forget that the other person may have a hidden agenda, or that he or she may be unconsciously engaging in transference or projection.

13

•••••

Activities: Communications and Closure

Communications that are clear, direct, and open reduce or eliminate misunderstandings, allow for genuineness and honesty in communications, promote trust, address the fear the receiver may have of hidden agendas, and are a way of taking personal responsibility for personal thoughts and feelings.

It is relatively easy to have misunderstandings about what was said and what was meant when communications are not direct and open. For example, indirect communications can permit the speaker to change his or her intended meaning when challenged by the receiver, or someone disagrees. This situation then puts the receiver in the position of being chastised for misunderstanding when, in fact, he or she did understand. This is a dishonest way to communicate, and does not foster trust development.

It is not unusual for speakers and receivers to use the same words that can have different meanings, and not realize that they are talking about different things. For example, what do the terms *next weekend* and *this weekend* mean to you? For some, "this weekend" is the forthcoming one while for others it is the one that just passed. Lots of confusion could result if plans were to be made and there was this misunderstanding. This is a relatively mild example. Consider how much more important this confusion is in your important relationships.

The following table presents some common situations that can occur in groups and in other relationships where indirect and closed communication can occur and is ineffective. Each is accompanied by an example of a more effective communication that is direct and open.

Closed, Indirect, and Ineffective Communication	Direct, Open, and Effective Communication
You shouldn't apologize.	When you apologize for something like you just did, I feel _____.
You aren't hearing me.	From your response, it doesn't feel that you heard or understood what I said or my feelings.
You seem to have a lot of suppressed feelings in this group.	I suppress many feelings.
What are we supposed to be doing?	I'm confused and anxious.
Are we doing it right?	I need some assurance and certainty. I feel really unsafe in unknown and ambiguous situations.

• • • • •

Make Personal Statements

Speak for yourself. Do not presume to speak for others. When you use "we" instead of "I" you are not taking responsibility for the feeling or thought you are expressing. By putting the expression in collective terms you are trying to diffuse perceived potentials for criticism or blame. It can also be a less than honest way to express something you think or feel that you fear could be perceived by the receiver as offensive, rejecting, blaming, critical, unflattering, or the like, and you do not want to be held accountable for the feelings you have.

Some excuses people give for failing to make personal statements incorporate a desire not to offend another person. This desire is also generally accompanied by an unspoken belief that the other person is unable to take care of him- or herself and, must be protected from the speaker's aggression, power, or destructiveness. That stance can be a bit grandiose. Yes, you can say something that is offensive. However, even the most negative comment can be accepted when it is phrased as a personal statement about your thoughts or feelings. However, do not think that, just because you say "I think" or "I feel," it is a personal statement. When saying "I think" or "I feel" is followed by a "you are" phrase, it is not a personal statement; it is a disguised and indirect way of pointing the finger of blame or criticism at the other person. If you can take responsibility for what you think and feel, you will not likely be offensive, rejecting, and so on, nor will the other person perceive what you say as blaming or criticizing unless old parental messages are triggered for him or her. When that happens, the other person is responsible for his or her triggered feelings. Some examples of personal versus nonpersonal statements follow.

Nonpersonal Statements	Personal Statements
I think you are resisting.	I felt you pull away when ___ was proposed.
I feel we are talking about trivia.	I have something important to discuss.
I feel you are suppressing with you as I feelings.	I'd like you to tell me what's going on think it could be something important.
I think we all agree that _____.	I think, or feel, that _____.
The group talked about important things in the session.	I talked, (or did not talk) about something important to me in this session

When you take responsibility for your feelings and thoughts you are less likely to offend the other person as he or she can accept that what you are expressing is your feeling. That is, unless you are trying to manipulate, intimidate, or seduce in an indirect way. If any of these are your motives, then you are not being genuine and that is destructive to forming and maintaining relationships.

● ● ● ● ●

Constructive Feedback

Measures of trust, safety, and cohesion for the relationships in the group rely on the willingness of members to give and receive feedback. This of course, assumes that the feedback is constructive. All feedback is not constructive and guidelines for constructive feedback are presented later in the discussion.

Constructive feedback can be telling a member how you perceive him or her; verbalizing your reactions to what someone is saying; giving praise and encouragement; describing what nonverbal behaviors accompanied the person's verbal behaviors, especially when there was dissonance; describing what a member did or said that irritated, offended, or turned you off, but also taking responsibility for your feelings; and pointing out a member's strengths.

Feedback is not used to put someone down or put them in their place, point out how you are superior, to tell the other person "off," infer their motives for what they are doing and saying, or as an indirect expression of hostility.

● ● ● ● ●

Guidelines for Constructive Feedback

Constructive feedback has certain characteristics, the most important of which is that it is information about the receiver that he or she can use in helpful ways; it is focused on observable behavior; careful selection of words; a sharing of information; and attending to the impact of the feedback on the receiver. The following guidelines can help ensure that the provider of the feedback is making it constructive.

Focus on observable behavior rather than inferring motives for what the person is doing helps to provide a reality check and reduce possible defensiveness. Observable behavior can also provide consensual validation by other group members that others also observed that behavior.

Choose words that are specific and descriptive of the behavior and of the sender's reactions. For example, it is not helpful to tell someone that a change in his or her attitude is in order. It can be helpful to tell someone that a behavior produces some feelings for you because you have a different perception of that person. An example would be hearing someone make depreciating or denigrating comments about him- or herself, and you tell the person that when you hear those comments it produces sadness for you as that person appears to be overlooking many positive personal characteristics that you've observed.

Sharing information is very different from saying or inferring that someone should or ought to know or do something, or giving the person some advice. When information is shared, it is presented in such a way that respects the other person, the provider accepts responsibility for what he or she is saying, and is not insisting that the other person has to agree with the provider. While wanting to be helpful by giving someone the benefit of personal past experience, or other knowledge, giving advice is seldom helpful, and is more likely to arouse irritation and defensiveness. Giving advice also sends a message that the giver is in some way superior to the receiver which does not help the relationship.

Limiting the amount of information and staying in touch with the impact on the other person is critical. Do not try to give all of the information you think the other person needs, limit the amount to what the other person can take in and use. This is especially important when there is some sensitivity or emotional intensity because the receiver can only deal with so much at any given time. Also, be sure to observe the impact of what is being conveyed on the receiver, and be prepared to stop when the emotional intensity appears to increase. You do not want to overwhelm the receiver because this can produce resistance, and defensiveness.

Above all, when providing feedback, please remember that the needs and feelings of the receiver are more important than those of the provider. The receiver can be very vulnerable and can easily feel on the hot seat, or attacked.

Exercise 13.1 Was It Constructive?

Materials: A sheet of paper and a pen or pencil for each group member. A suitable hard surface for writing.

Procedure:

1. Tell group members that feedback can be constructive or destructive, and to think of a recent time when they received feedback from someone.

2. Have them write a brief description of the situation that includes the person, place, time of day or month, the information the person tried to convey (feedback), and his or her reaction.

3. Tell members to reflect on the experience and to list all of the feelings experienced then and now as they reflect and write about it.

4. Ask them to make a judgment as to whether the feedback was constructive or not constructive.

5. Reconvene the group in a circle, and ask them to share their feelings and judgments. If members want to share their summaries, limit this to the summary and a few minutes. Try not to let them get into details.

6. Have members write a brief paragraph as to how the feedback they received could have been constructive if it was not. This too can be shared in the group.

● ● ● ● ●

Receiving Feedback

Receiving feedback can be difficult at times because of the emotional involvement with the topic or issue. In addition, the receiver may have experienced blaming, criticism, or other emotional abuse under the guise of "just trying to help," "just trying to keep you from making a mistake." Old parental messages and other experiences can intervene to cause the receiver to be mistrustful, cautious, defensive, or wary when receiving feedback. All these possible member conditions are why sufficient trust and safety have to be developed before members are able to give and receive feedback that is perceived as constructive. The perception of the receiver is important. The motives of the giver may be positive, but the receiver has to feel they are positive in order to accept and use the feedback. Because past experiences play an important role in the ability to perceive feedback as constructive, it can be important to remember this possibility when receiving feedback. Teaching group members how to manage receiving feedback can be helpful. For example, tell them that when they find that they are becoming defensive, resistant, and the like, to mentally detach and examine if their reaction is based on past experiences and people more than on present experiences and people.

How can you tell if you are being defensive? If your reaction is one or more of the following, you are defensive, and possibly resistant.

- A desire to retaliate;
- Rejection of what the person says without any consideration of its merits or validity;
- A sarcastic response;
- Immediate denial;
- Hurt feelings;
- Resentment or anger;
- Change or deflection of topic.

Accepting feedback does not mean agreeing with what the person says. It does mean that what was said and meant was also heard and understood, and there is a willingness or openness to considering the feedback as possibly being valid. The receiver may still end up disagreeing, but only after a careful examination. The best kind of feedback leaves the receiver free to accept any or all of it, or conclude that it does not fit. The most important outcome is that the relationship is not damaged, but rather is strengthened. Both the receiver and the giver of the feedback feel positive about what was said, and about the relationship.

Exercise 13.2 Accepting Feedback

Materials: A sheet of paper for each group member, and a pen or pencil. A large sheet of newsprint with the list of defensive behaviors described above, such as anger and a sarcastic response, written on it, and masking tape for posting the list.

Procedure:

1. Distribute the materials and ask group members to think of a time when they received feedback and became defensive. Refer them to the posted list of responses.

2. Have them write a brief description of the event, the people involved, the setting, and all of the feelings they experienced. Give about 10 minutes for the writing.

3. Reconvene the group and ask members to share what they wrote, or the list of feelings they experienced. Be sure to ask if those same feelings and the intensity were triggered by remembering the event.

4. Ask members to identify what the sender said or did that produced the defensiveness; tone of voice, choice of words, inappropriate venue, the sender seemed to infer blame or criticism, and the like.

5. Now, ask members to reflect on the feelings and how they perceived the sender, and to try and visualize how events could or would have played out if they had not become defensive, and to write a brief paragraph about what emerged. For example, what do they think would have happened for them and for the receiver if they had been willing to consider some or all of the feedback as possibly being valid? Ask members to share any part of what emerged for them as they reflected and wrote.

6. Hold a discussion on members' characteristic way of behaving and feeling when receiving feedback, and if they can think of more appropriate or constructive ways to receive feedback.

● ● ● ● ●

Constructive Conflict and Conflict Resolution

The group leader's attitude about conflict is a major contributor to how the leader will manage conflict both in and out of the group, and the same is true for group members. Common attitudes about conflict include the following:

■ Fear conflict as experience has shown it to be distressing and destructive.

■ Avoid or overlook conflict in the hope that it will go away

■ Almost always try to bring harmony and soothe disagreements so as not to feel the distress.

■ Change personal thoughts and attitudes to agree with the other person so that conflict does not emerge.

■ Restrict expressing thoughts and feelings out of concern that they may produce conflict.

■ Rationalize or intellectualize an unwillingness to acknowledge that conflict exists.

When the group leader has any or all of these, he or she is overlooking a rich source of energy for relationship building, and failing to use the opportunity to teach members how to manage their thoughts and feelings when they are in a conflict situation.

These attitudes could be a result of past unpleasant experiences around conflicts. Some people may even have an erroneous perception that conflicts are fights and are always destructive, or can equate conflict with actual or potential violence. These attitudes and perceptions can lead some people to react to conflict or potential conflict by thinking that it their responsibility to make sure there are no disagreements, or to smooth over any that appear. These are all counterproductive attitudes and behaviors whether for the leader or for the members. The group experience can be an opportunity for both parties to examine and modify these attitudes, and to experiment with more constructive conflict behaviors.

Exercise 13.3 How I Perceive Conflicts

Materials: A sheet of paper with the following terms on it for each member. Put all of the terms in one long list. A pen or pencil for writing.

1. Distribute the materials and introduce the exercise.
2. Tell members that the first step is to select all the terms that they feel describes conflict for them. They can choose as many as you wish.

collision	disagreement	contradictory
at variance with	opposition	clash
contend	battle	struggle
strife	controversy	quarrel
discord	antagonism	incompatibility
opposition	fight	discrepancy

3. The next step is to make a list of all associations they have for the concept of conflict. Just think about the term and allow the associations to emerge. Don't try to edit or change them, just record what emerged.
4. Review the terms and associations. Put a + sign beside all positive associations, and a – sign beside all that are negative. If they have some terms they consider to be neutral; put a 0 beside those. Add the positives, negatives, and zeros separately. Which category has the most associations: positive, negative, or neutral?

The tendency to consider conflicts as positive, negative, or neutral will impact how the person perceives and behaves around conflict situations. The more positive associations they have, the better able they will be to recognize conflicts, be willing to work through them, and be able to tolerate feelings connected to them, whether the feelings are their own or the feelings of others. The more someone tends to have negative associations, the less able that person will be to recognize conflict in its early stages and to accept that conflict does exist. These people will be more willing to use defense mechanisms, such as repression, denial, rationalization, and intellectualization; and to engage in behaviors that are designed to deflect any open consideration of conflict. It must be emphasized that the attitudes and behaviors around negative associations are not "wrong" or "bad"; they are a realization or awareness that provides material that could be productive if explored.

Exercise 13.4 A Conflict Resolution Process

Materials: Sheets of paper and a pen or pencil for writing.

Procedure:

1. Distribute the materials and ask group members to think of a recent or past conflict they experienced, and to write a brief description of it.

2. Next, have them define the conflict as they perceive it: a clash of opinions, a clash of values, a misunderstanding or errors of fact, or a clash of interests where there is high emotional intensity for that group member.

3. Have them repeat step 2 for other people in the conflict; that is, how do they perceive how the other person defines the conflict.

4. Next, ask them to list all of the feelings they are experiencing as they think and write about the conflict and to rate the emotional intensity for each as: 5—extremely high; 4—very high; 3—some distress; 2—little distress; or 1—no distress. Also, have them list and rate the other person's feelings as they perceive them.

5. Have members write what they would consider to be a satisfactory outcome, and whether that is a realistic possibility, especially if it calls for capitulation or change on the other person's part.

6. Ask them to write a brief paragraph about the conflict as they perceive it, and the feelings they have after working through steps 1 to 5. Have them rate whether their feelings are still as high as in step 4, or if the feelings have become less intense.

7. Hold a brief discussion about what members have experienced to this point. Keep the discussion brief, focused on feelings, and whether step 5 could be revisited and revised.

● ● ● ● ●

Termination and Closure

It can be particularly difficult to provide adequate termination and closure for many challenging groups since some, such as open and self-help groups do not have definitive ending dates. Termination and closure are easier to present for other types of groups such as many closed groups, but some challenging groups are more likely to have individual member terminations which means that group leaders need to prepare and facilitate the member's termination and that for the remaining group members. Thus, there are five situations where a group leader will have to manage termination and closure:

- When the entire group will leave, such as what occurs for the planned single session group.
- Individual member termination, planned (see chapter 6).
- Individual member termination, unplanned (see chapter 6).
- The remaining group members when a group member terminates, planned (see chapter 6).
- The remaining group members when there is premature termination for a member (see chapters 6 and 10).

The importance for orderly and potentially satisfying termination and closure should not be minimized or underestimated as this provides opportunities for members to express the many reactions and feelings that they may have. Further, they can experience or experiment with more constructive and satisfying ways to end relationships and this learning can be carried over to their lives outside of the group. An additional consideration is for the members who remain in the group when a member terminates, either planned or unplanned. The group leader can expect that the group will be different in some way, and that the remaining group members can also need to express their thoughts and feelings about the terminating member, and how the group will then differ. This can be especially important in the face of an unplanned premature termination where the group is left in doubt about the reason for the termination, and can feel that the group contributed to that member's leaving.

Major goals and purposes for planned termination and closure include the following:

- Review and assess personal goal accomplishments.
- Verbalize major learning, awareness, and understandings that were acquired.
- Provide feedback to group members and to the leader about how they were experienced in the group. This can also be another source for further learning.
- Express feelings of loss and grief some members can have about the group, and about the relationships that are ending.
- Experience a constructive and satisfying process for saying good-bye, or for ending relationships.

The activities presented here fall into three categories: individual, group, planned or unplanned. The activities presented for individual member termination can usually be modified to be used when a group ends by extending the task to include all group members, not just the one(s) who are terminating. The group focused activities here are intended for use with the remaining group members when one or more members terminate, either planned or unplanned. Presented first are the activities for individual member termination.

● ● ● ● ●

Individual

Exercise 13.5 Leave-Taking

Materials: None

Procedure:

1. Introduce the exercise by announcing or reminding the group that a member is leaving, and this will be an opportunity to say good-bye. Describe the process as follows: (a) each group member is asked to tell the leaving member how he or she was experienced in the group; for example, saying that the person was experienced as being responsible and working hard; (b) when the group members are finished, the leaving member is asked to tell each member how he or she experienced that person in the group.

2. The same process is used to have members report on their feelings about the departure, and to give the terminating member a personal wish for the future; and vice versa.

Exercise 13.6 Appreciation and Wishes

Materials: A small box or bag large enough to contain strips of paper, one from each member; strips of colored paper, two or more for each member; and a pen or pencil for writing. Note: members can be asked to prepare the strips before the group begins.

Procedure:

1. Spread the materials out, and ask group members to select two or more strips of paper and a pen or pencil.

2. Ask them to write something they appreciate about the member who is leaving on one strip, and to write a wish for that person on the other strip.

3. Collect all the strips, place them in the bag, and present it to the leaving member at the end of the session.

4. Have a group discussion on feelings that emerged as they wrote on the strips, as they think about that member leaving, and their perceptions of how the group may be different. Ask the leaving member to talk about his or her feelings about leaving, and about the group.

Group—Planned

Exercise 13.7 Colors and Symbols

Materials: A sheet of paper for each member, a set of crayons, or colored pencils, or felt markers for each member; and a suitable surface for drawing and writing.

Procedure:

1. Distribute the materials and tell group members that there can be numerous feelings that emerge about the group as it prepares to end.
2. Ask them to draw lines on the sheet of paper to divide it into four sections; and to let themselves become aware of the major feelings they have as they reflect on the group experience, and the group's ending.
3. Next, ask them to select one color and draw a symbol for one feeling. Then, move to the next quadrant and do the same for another feeling they may have. Repeat this for the other two quadrants.
4. Reconvene the group in a circle and ask members to share their symbols and colors.
5. Discuss how members felt as they reflected, drew, and shared.

Exercise 13.8 A Group Seal

Materials: A large sheet of newsprint paper (16" × 20" or larger) with a large circle drawn on it that fills up the page, a sheet of paper for each group member, pens or pencils for writing, masking tape for posting the newsprint, and a set of felt markers.

Procedure:

1. Introduce the exercise by telling members that the group is ending, and that each has a perception or image of the group. The task is to prepare a group seal that incorporates all of the members' perceptions and images.
2. Ask members to use the paper and pencils or pens and to write down all of the thoughts, feelings, and associations that come to mind as

they reflect on the group, how they experienced the group and its members, and about the group's ending.

3. Next, ask members to review their lists and to allow an overall impression or image of the group to emerge.

4. Each member is to select one or more markers and draw on the posted circle, what emerged for step 3.

5. Post the seal after every group member has contributed, and reconvene the group in a circle.

6. Ask members to go around and speak of their reactions to the posted seal.

7. Hold a discussion about what emerged for them in step 2, and note similarities among members. Also discuss the feelings they have about the group and its ending.

References   • • • • •

Agazarian, Y. (1997). *Systems-centered therapy for groups.* New York, NY: Guilford.

Ahmadi, K. (2007). What is a self-help group? Psych Central.com/lib/2007

Alonso, A., & Rutan, J. S. (1996). Separation and individuation in the group leader. *International Journal of Group Psychotherapy, 46,* 149–162.

Ainsworth, M. (2008). E-therapy: History and survey. From metanoia.org/imhs/history.

Andersen, R. M. (1995a). Behavioral model of families' use of health services research (Series No. 25). Chicago, IL: Center for Health Administration Studies, University of Chicago. (Original work published 1968)

Andersen, R. M. (1995b). Revisiting the behavioral model and access to medical care: Does it matter? *Journal of Health and Social Behavior, 36,* 1–10. (Original work published 1968)

Ardito, R., & Rahellino, D. (2011, October 18). Therapeutic alliance and outcome of psychotherapy: Historical excursus, measurements and prospects for research. *Frontier Psychology.* doi: wo.3389/fpsyg.2011.00270

Astrachan, B. Harrow, M., Becker, R., Swartz, A., & Miller, J. (1967). The unled patient groups as a therapeutic tool. *International Journal of Group Psychotherapy, 17,* 178–191.

Baekeland, F., & Lundwall, L. (1975). Dropping out of treatment: A critical review. *Psychological Bulletin, 82*(5), 738–783. doi: http://dx.doi.org/10.1037/h0077132

Beck, A. (2000). *Cognitive therapy.* New York, NY: Guilford.

Becu, M., Becu, N., Manzur, G., & Kochen, S. (1993). Self-help epilepsy groups: An evaluation of effect on depression and schizophrenia. *Epilepsia, 34*(5), 841–843.

Binder, J., & Strupp, H. (1997). "Negative process": A recurrently discovered and underestimated facet of therapeutic process and outcome in the individual psychotherapy of adults. *Clinical Psychology: Science and Practice, 4,* 121–139.

Bion, W. (1961). *Experiences in groups.* New York: Basic Books.

Boisvert, C., & Faust, D. (2006). Practicing psychologists' knowledge of general psychotherapy research findings: Implications for science-practice relations. *Professional Psychology: Research and Practice, 37,* 708–715.

Bonhote, K., Romano-Egan, J., & Cornwell, C. (1999). Altruism and creative expression in a long-term older adult psychotherapy group. *Issues in Mental Health Nursing, 20,* 603–617.

Bordin, E. (1979). The generalizability of the psychoanalytic concept of the working alliance. *Psychotherapy (Chic.), 16,* 252–260.

Borman, L. (1992). Introduction: Self-help/mutual aid groups in strategies for health. In A. Katz, H. Hendrick, D. Isenberg, L. Thompson, T. Goodrich, & A. Kutschen (Eds.), *Self help: Concepts and applications* (pp. 1–27). Philadelphia, PA: Charles Press.

Bowlby, J. (1988). *A secure base: Clinical applications of attachment theory.* London: Routledge & Kegan Paul.

Brandes, N., & Todd, D. (1972). Dissolution of a peer supervision group of individual psychotherapists. *International Journal of Group Psychotherapy, 22,* 54–59.

Brown, N. (2003a). Conceptualizing process. *International Journal of Group Psychotherapy, 53*(2), 225–243.

Brown, N. (2003b). *Psychoeducational groups: Process and practice* (2nd ed.). New York, NY: Brunner-Routledge.

Brown, N. (2006). Reconceptualizing difficult groups and difficult members. *Journal of Contemporary Psychotherapy, 36*(3), 145–150.

Brown, N. (2009). *Becoming a group leader.* Upper Saddle River, NJ: Pearson Education.

Brown, N. (2011). *Psychoeducational groups* (3rd ed.). New York, NY: Routledge.

Brown, N. (2012). *Creative activities for group therapy.* New York, NY: Routledge.

Brown, W., Consedine, N., & Magai, C. (2005). Altruism relates to health in an ethnically diverse sample of older adults. *Journal of Gerontology, 60B*(3), 143–152.

Cameron, L., Booth, R., Schlatter, M., Ziginskas, D., & Harman, J. (2007). Changes in emotion regulation and psychological adjustment following use of a group psychosocial support program for women recently diagnosed with breast cancer. *Psycho-oncology, 16*(3), 171–180.

Campo, R. (2003). *The healing art: A doctor's black bag of poetry.* New York, NY: W.W. Norton.

Castera, M., & Lund, D. (1993). Intrapersonal resources and the effectiveness of self-help groups for bereaved older adults. *Gerontologist, 33*(5), 619–629.

Castonguay, L., Pincus, A., Agras, W., & Hines, C. (1998). The role of emotion in group cognitive behavioral therapy for binge eating disorders: When things have to feel worse before they get better. *Psychotherapy Research, 8,* 225–238.

Castonguay, L., Schut, A., Aikins, D, Constantino, M., Laurenceau, J., Bologh, L., & Burns, D. (2004). Integrative cognitive therapy for depression: A preliminary investigation. *Journal of Psychotherapy Integration, 14,* 4–20.

Cialdini, R., Darbey, K., & Vincent, J. (1973). Transgression and altruism: A case for hedonism. *Journal of Experimental and Social Psychology, 9,* 502–516.

Cook, J., Heller, T., & Pickett-Schenk, S. A. (1999). The effect of support group participation on caregiver burden among parents of adult offspring with severe mental illness. *Family Relations, 48,* 405–410.

Corey, G. (2008). *Theory and practice of group counseling* (7th ed.). Belmont, CA: Thompson, Brooks/Cole.

Counselman, E. (1991). Leadership in a long-term leaderless women's group. *Small Group Research, 22*(2), 240–257.

Coyne, R., Crowill, J., & Newmeyer, M. (2008). *Group techniques: How to use them more purposefully.* Upper Saddle River, NJ: Pearson Education.

Crandall, J. (1984). Social interest as a moderator of life stress. *Journal of Personality and Social Psychology, 47,* 164–174.

Crits-Christoph, P., Gibbons, P., & Connolly, M. (2002). Relational interpretations. In J. C. Norcross (Ed.), *Psychotherapy relationships that work: Therapist contributions and responsiveness to patients* (pp. 285–300). New York, NY: Oxford University Press.

Crits-Christoph, P., Gibbons, M, Crits-Christoph, K., Narduci, J., Schamberger, M., & Gallop, R. (2006). Can therapists be trained to improve their alliances: A preliminary study of alliance-fostering psychotherapy. *Psychotherapy Research, 16*, 268–281.

Desmond, R., & Seligman, M. (1977). A review of research on leaderless groups. *Small Group Research, 8*(1), 3–24.

Dimidjian, W., & Hollon, S. (2010). How would we know if psychotherapy were harmful? *American Psychologist, 65*(1), 21–33.

Emrick, D., & Tonigna, J. (1993). Alcoholics Anonymous: What is currently known? In B. McCrady & W. Miller (Eds.), *Research on Alcoholics Anonymous: Opportunities and alternatives* (pp. 41–75). New Brunswick, NJ: Rutgers Center of Alcohol Studies.

Forsyth, D. (1999). *Group dynamics* (3rd ed.). Pacific Grove, CA: Brooks/Cole.

Galanter, M. (1988). Zealous self-help groups as adjuncts to psychiatric treatment: A study of Recovery, Inc. *American Journal of Psychiatry, 145*, 1248–1253.

Gans, J., & Alonso, A. (1998). Difficult patients: Their construction in group therapy. *International Journal of Group Psychotherapy, 48*(3), 311–326.

Garfield, S. (1978). Research on client variables in psychotherapy. In A. E. Bergin & S. L. Garfield (Eds.), *Handbook of psychotherapy and behavior change* (2nd ed., pp. 191–231). New York, NY: Wiley.

Garfield, S. (1994). Research on client variables in psychotherapy. In A. E. Bergin & S. L. Garfield (Eds.), *Handbook of psychotherapy and behavior change* (4th ed., pp. 270–387). New York, NY: Wiley.

Gartner, A., & Reissman, F. (Eds.). (1977). *Self-help in the human services.* San Francisco, CA: Jossey-Bass.

Gelso, C., & Hayes, J. (2007). *Countertransference and the therapist's inner experience: Perils and possibilities.* Mahwah, NJ: Erlbaum.

Gilden, J., & Hendrys, M. (1992). Diabetes support groups improve health care of older diabetic patients. *Journal of the American Geriatrics Society, 40*, 147–150.

Gladding, S. (2003). *Group work: A counseling specialty* (4th ed.). Upper Saddle River, NJ: Merrill/Prentice Hall.

Green, L., Meisler, A., Pilkey, D., Alexander, G., Cardella, L., Sirois, B., & Burg, M. (2004). Psychological work with groups in the Veterans Administration. In J. DeLucia-Waack, D. Gerrity, C. Kalodner, & M. Riva (Eds.), *Handbook of group counseling and psychotherapy* (pp. 317–340). Thousand Oaks, CA: Sage.

Greenson, R. (1965). The working alliance and the transference neuroses. *Psychoanalytic Quarterly, 34*, 155–179.

Gruner, L. (1984). Membership composition of open and closed therapeutic groups. *Small Group Research, 15*(2), 222–232. doi: 10.1177/104646964 8401500205.

Hafen, B., Karren, K., Frandsen, J., & Smith, N. (1996). *Mind/body health.* New York, NY: Guilford.

Hall, S. (2012). *Using the Counseling Center Assessment of Psychological Symptoms-34 (CCAPS-34) to predict premature termination in a college counseling center sample* (Unpublished dissertation). Old Dominion University, Norfolk, VA.

Hatfield, E., Cacioppo, J., & Rapson, R. (1994). *Emotional contagion.* New York, NY: Cambridge University Press.

Hinrichsen, G., & Reversol, T. (1985). Does self-help help? An empirical investigation of scoliosis peer support groups. *Journal of Social Issues, 41*(1), 65–87.

Holmes, J., & Cureton, E. (1970). Group therapy interaction with and without the leader. *Journal of Social Psychology, 81,* 127–130.

Holmes, S., & Kivlighan, D. (2000). Comparison of therapeutic factors in group and individual treatment processes. *Journal of Counseling Psychology, 47,* 478–484. doi: 10.1037/0022-0167.47.4.478.

Holton, C. (1995). Once upon a time served: Therapeutic application of fairy tales within a correctional environment. *International Journal of Offender Therapy and Comparative Criminology, 39*(3), 210–221.

Hopper, E. (2001). On the nature of hope in psychoanalysis and group analysis. *British Journal of Psychotherapy, 18* (2), 1–21.

Horvath, A. (2000). The therapeutic relationship: From transference to alliance. *Journal of Clinical Psychology, 56,* 163–173.

Horvath, A., & Bedi, R. (2002). The alliance. In J. Norcross (Ed.), *Psychotherapy relationships that work: Therapist contributions and responsiveness to patients* (pp. 37–69). New York, NY: Oxford University Press.

Horvath, A., & Luborsky, L. (1993). The role of the therapeutic alliance in psycho-therapy. *Journal of Consulting and Clinical Psychology, 61,* 561–573. doi: 1037/0022-006x.61.4.561

Horvath, A., & Symonds, B. (1991). Relation between working alliance and outcome in psychotherapy: A meta-analysis. *Journal of Counseling Psychology, 38,* 139–149. doi:10.1037/0022-0167.38.2.139

Humphreys, K., Mavis, B., & Stoffelmayr, B. (1994). Are twelve step programs appropriate for disenfranchised groups? Evidence for a study of post-treatment mutual help involvement. *Prevention in Human Services, 11*(1), 165–179.

Humphreys, K., & Moos, R. (1996). Reduced substance-abuse related costs among voluntary participants in Alcoholics Anonymous. *Psychiatric Services, 47,* 709–713.

Humphreys, K., & Moos, R. (2001). Can encouraging substance abuse patients to participate in self-help groups reduce demand for health care? A quasi-experimental study. *Alcoholism: Clinical and Experimental Research, 25,* 711–716.

Hunt, W., & Issacharoff, A. (1975). History and analysis of a leaderless group of professional therapists. *American Journal of Psychiatry, 132,* 1164–1167.

Hurst, J., Delworth, U., & Garriott, R. (1973). Encounter-tapes: Evaluation of a leaderless group procedure. *Small Group Behavior, 4,* 476–485.

Jacobs, E., Masson, R., & Harvill, R. (2009). *Group counseling* (6th ed.). Pacific Grove, CA: Brooks/Cole.

Johnson, D. (2003). *Reaching out* (8th ed.). Boston, MA: Allyn & Bacon.

Johnson, D., & Johnson, F. (2006). *Joining together* (8th ed.). Boston, MA: Allyn & Bacon.

Karver, M., Jandelsman, J., Fields, S., & Bickman, L. (2006). Meta-analysis of the therapeutic relationship variables in youth and family therapy: The evidence for different relationship variables in the child and adolescent treatment outcome literature. *Clinical Psychology Review, 26,* 50–65. doi:1016/j.cpr.2005.09.001.

Katz, H. (1993). *Self-help in America: A social movement perspective.* New York, NY: Twayne.

Kazdin, A., Holland, L., & Crowley, M. (1997). Family experience of barriers to treatment and premature termination from child therapy. *Journal of Consulting and Clinical Psychology, 65*(3), 453–463. doi: 10.1037/0022-006X.65.3.453

Kazdin, A., & Wassell, G. (2000). Predictors of barriers to treatment and therapeutic change in outpatient therapy for antisocial children and their families. *Mental Health Services Research, 2*, 27–40.

Kennedy, M. (1990, July). *Psychiatric hospitalization of GROWers.* Paper presented at the Second Biennial Conference on Community Research and Action. East Lansing MI.

Kessler, R. C., Mikelson, K. D., & Zhao, S. (1997). Patterns and correlated of self-help group members in the United States. *Social Policy, 27*, 27–46.

Kivlighan, D., Coleman, M., & Anderson, D. (2000). Process, outcome and methodology in group counseling research. In S. D. Brown & R. W. Lent (Eds.), *Handbook of counseling psychology* (3rd ed., pp. 767–796). New York, NY: Wiley.

Kivlighan, D. Jr., & Goldfine, D. C. (1991). Endorsement of therapeutic factors as a function of group development and participant interpersonal attitudes. *Journal of Counseling Psychology, 38*, 150–158.

Kivlighan, D., & Holmes, S. (2004). The importance of therapeutic factors. In J. DeLucia-Waack, D. Gerrity, C. Kalodner, & M. Rina (Eds.), *Handbook of group counseling and psychotherapy.* Thousand Oaks CA: Sage.

Kivlighan, D. M. Jr., & Mulligan, R. (1988). Participant's perception of therapeutic factors in group counseling. The role of interpersonal style and stage of group development. *Small Group Behavior, 19*, 452–468.

Kline, F. (1972). Dynamics of a leaderless group. *International Journal of Group Psychotherapy, 22*, 234–242.

Kline, G. (1974). Terminating a leaderless group. *International Journal of Group Psychotherapy, 24*, 452–459.

Kohut, H. (1977). *The restoration of the self.* Madison, CT: International Universities Press.

Kurtz, L. (1988). Mutual aid for affective disorders: The manic depressive and depressive association. *American Journal of Orthopsychiatry, 58*(1), 152–155.

Kyrouz, E., Humphreys, K., & Loomis, C. (2007). A review of research on the effectiveness of self-help groups. In B. White & E. Madars (Eds.), *American self-help clearinghouse sourcebook* (7th ed., chapter 5). Denville NJ: American Self-Help Group Clearinghouse, St. Clare's Health Services.

Langdon, S., & Petracca, G. (2010). Tiny dancer: Body image and dancer identity in female modern dancers. *Body Image, 7*(4), 360–363.

Leszcz, M. (2012, March). *Activating the here and now: Integrating the existential and the interpersonal in group therapy.* Special Institute presentation at the American Group Psychotherapy Association Conference, New York, NY.

Lewin, K. (1944). Dynamics of group action. *Educational Leadership, 1*(4), 195–200.

Lewin, K. (1951). *Field theory in social science.* New York, NY: Harper.

Lewin, K., Lippitt, R., & White, R. (1939). Conduct, knowledge, and acceptance of new values. *Journal of Social Psychology, 10*, 271–299.

Lieberman, M., & Videka-Sherman, L. (1986). The impact of self-help groups on the mental health of widows and widowers. *American Journal of Orthopsychiatry, 56*(3), 435–449.

Lilienfeld, S. (2007). Psychological treatments that cause harm. *Perspectives on Psychological Science, 2,* 53–70.

Linehan, M. (1993). *Cognitive-behavioral therapy for borderline personality disorder.* New York, NY: Guilford.

Luoh, M., & Herzog, A. (2002). Individual consequences of volunteer and paid work in old age: Health and mortality. *Health and Social Behavior, 43,* 490–509.

MacKenzie, K. (1990). *Introduction to time-limited group therapy.* Washington, DC: American Psychiatric Press.

Marmar, C., & Horwitz, M. (1988). A controlled trial of brief psychotherapy and mutual self-help group treatment of conjugal bereavement. *American Journal of Psychiatry, 145*(2), 203–209.

Martin, D., Garske, J., & Davis, M. (2000). Relation of the therapeutic alliance with outcome and other variables: A meta-analytic review. *Journal of Consulting and Clinical Psychology, 68,* 438–450.

McAuliffe, W., (1990). A randomized controlled trial of recovery training and self-help for opioid addicts in New England and Hong Kong. *Journal of Psychoactive Drugs, 22*(2), 197–209.

McKay, J., & Alterman, A. (1994). Treatment goals, continuity of care and outcome in a day hospital substance abuse rehabilitation program. *American Journal of Psychiatry, 151*(2), 254–259.

Meichenbaum, D. (1977). *Cognitive-behavior modification: An integrative approach.* New York, NY: Plenum.

Midlarsky, E. (1991). Helping as coping. In M. S. Clark (Ed.), *Prosocial behavior* (pp. 238–264). Thousand Oaks, CA: Sage.

Miller, M., Denton, G., & Tobacyk, J. (1986). Social interest and feelings of hopelessness among elderly people. *Psychological Reports, 58,* 410.

Mullan, F. (1992). Rewriting the social contract in health. In A. Katz, H. Hendrick, D. Isenberg, L. Thompson, T. Goodrich, & A. Kutscher (Eds.), *Self-help concepts and applications* (pp. 61–68). Philadelphia, PA: Charles Press.

Nask, K., & Dramer, K. (1992). Self-help for sickle cell disease in African American communities. *Journal of Applied Behavioral Science, 19*(2), 201–215.

National Multiple Sclerosis Society. (2010). *Best practices leaders manual.* New York, NY: Author.

Norcross, J. (2002). *Psychotherapy relationships that work: Therapist contributions and responsiveness to patients.* New York, NY: Oxford University Press.

Ohnmeiss, D., Vanharanta, H., & Elkholm, J. (1999). Relationship of pain drawings to invasive tests assessing intervertebral disc pathology. *European Spine Journal, 8,* 126–131.

Owens, P., Hoagwood, K., Horwitz, S., Leaf, P., Poduska, M., Kellam, S., & Ialongo, N. (2002). Barriers to children's mental health services. *Journal of the American Academy of Child and Adolescent Psychiatry, 41,* 731–738.

Pekarik, G. (1985). Coping with dropouts. *Professional Psychology: Research and Practice, 16*(1), 114–123.

Pennebaker, J. W. (1997a). *Opening up: The healing power of expressing emotion.* New York, NY: Guilford.

Pennebaker, J. W. (1997b). Writing about emotional experiences as a therapeutic process. *Psychological Science, 8,* 162–166.

Pennebaker, J. (1999). Psychological factors influencing the reporting of physical

symptoms. In A. A. Stone, J. S. Turkan, C. A. Bachrach, J. B. Jobe, H. S. Kurtz-
man, & V. S. Cain (Eds.), *The science of self-report; Implications for research
and practice* (pp. 299–316). Mahwah, NJ: Erlbaum.

Phillips, E. (1987). The ubiquitous decay curve: Service delivery similarities in
psychotherapy, medicine, and addiction. *Professional Psychology: Research
and Practice, 18*(6), 650–652.

Posthuma, B. (2002). *Small groups in counseling and therapy*. Boston, MA: Allyn
& Bacon.

Potts, H. (2005). Online support groups: An overlooked resource for patients.
Retrieved from http://eprints.ucl.ac.uk/archive/00001406/01/Online support groups.pdu. University College of London.

Powell, T., Hill, E., Warner, L., Yeaton, W., & Silk, K. (2000). Encouraging people
with mood disorders to attend a self-help group. *Journal of Applied Social
Psychology, 39*, 2270–2288.

Roberts, L., Salem, D., Rappaport, J., Toto, P., Luke, D., & Seidman, E. (1999). Giving and receiving help: Interpersonal transactions in mutual-help meetings
and psychosocial adjustment of members. *American Journal of Community
Psychology, 27*, 841–868.

Rogers, C. (1951). *Client-centered therapy*. Boston, NY: Houghton Mifflin.

Rogers, C. (1979). *On encounter groups*. New York, NY: Harper & Row.

Rothaus, P., Morton, R., Johnson, D., Cleveland, S., & Lyle, F. (1963). Human relations training for psychiatric patients. *Archives of General Psychiatry, 8*,
572–581.

Rubenstein, G. (1970). *The impact of a leaderless group experience with elemen-
tary school teachers on class climate* (Unpublished doctoral dissertation).
University of Rochester, Rochester, NY.

Rutan, S., & Stone, W. (2001) *Psychodynamic group psychotherapy* (3rd ed.). New
York, NY: Guilford.

Salzberg, H. (1967). Verbal behavior in group psychotherapy with and without a
therapist. *Journal of Counseling Psychology, 14*, 24–27.

Schwartz, C., Meisenhelder, B., Ma, Y., & Reed, G. (2003). Altruistic social behaviors are associated with better mental health. *Psychosomatic Medicine, 65*,
778–785.

Seligman, M., & Desmond, R. (1975). The leaderless group phenomenon: A historical perspective. *International Journal of Group Psychotherapy, 25*, 277–290.

Seligman, M., & Sterne, D. (1969). Verbal behavior in therapist-led, leaderless, and
alternating group sessions. *Journal of Counseling Psychology, 16*, 320–328.

Shields, J., & Zander, K. (1985). *Peer consultation in a group context*. New York,
NY: Springer.

Shirk, S., & Karver, M. (2003). Predictions of treatment outcome from relationship variables in child and adolescent therapy: A meta-analytic
review. *Journal of Consulting and Clinical Psychology, 71*, 452–464.
doi:1037/002-006X.71.3–452.

Simons, R. (1971). *Intensity as a variable in programmed group interaction: The
marathon* (Unpublished Doctoral Dissertation). University of Utah, Salt
Lake City, UT.

Sterne, D., & Seligman, M. (1971). Further comparisons of verbal behavior in
therapist-led, leaderless, and alternating group psychotherapy sessions.
Journal of Counseling Psychology, 18, 472–477.

Strong, S. (1968). Counseling: An interpersonal influence process. *Journal of Counseling Psychology, 15*, 215–224.

Strupp, H. (2001). Implications of the empirically supported treatment movement for psychoanalysis. *Psychoanalytic Dialogues, 11*, 605–619. doi:10.1080/104818811 09348631

Subramanian, V., Stewart, M., & Smith, J. (1999). The development and impact of a chronic pain support group: A qualitative and quantitative study. *Journal of Pain and Symptom Management, 17*, 376–383.

Swift, J. K., & Callahan, J. (2010). A delay discounting model of psychotherapy termination. *International Journal of Behavioral Consultation and Therapy, 5*(3/4), 278–293. Retreived from EBSCOhost.

Toseland, R., Rossiter, C., & Labrecque, M. (1989, September). The effectiveness of two kinds of support groups for caregivers. *Social Service Review*, 415–432.

Truax, C., & Volksdorf, N. (1970). Antecendents to outcome in group counseling with institutionalized deliquents: Effects of therapeutic conditions, patient self-exploration, alternate sessions, and vicarious therapy pretraining. *Journal of Abnormal Psychology, 76*, 235–242.

Truax, C., Wargo, D., Carkuff, R. R., Kodman, F., & Moles, E. A. (1966). Changes in self-concept during group psychotherapy as a function of alternate sessions and viacarious therapy pretraining in institutionalized patients and juvenile deliquents. *Journal of Consulting Psychology, 30*, 309–314.

Tuckman, B. (1965). Developmental sequence in small groups. *Psychological Bulletin, 63*, 384–399.

Vachon, M., & Lyall, W. (1980). A controlled study of self-help interventions for widows. *American Journal of Psychiatry, 137*(11), 1380–1384.

Vicino, F., Krusell, J., Deci, E., & Landy, D. (1973). The impact of process: Self-administered exercises for personal and interpersonal development. *Journal of Applied Behavioral Science, 9*, 737–755.

Videka-Sherman, L., & Lieberman, M. (1985). The effects of self-help and psychotherapy intervention on child loss: The limits of recovery. *American Journal of Orthopsychiatry, 55*(1), 70–82.

Wampold, B. (2006). The psychotherapist. In J. Norcross, L. Beulter, & R. Levant (Eds.), *Evidence-based practices in mental health: Debate and dialogues on fundamental questions* (pp. 200–208). Washington, DC: American Psychological Association.

Watson, C., Hancock, M., Gearhart, Mendez, C., Malovrh, P., & Raden, M. (1997). A comparative outcome study of frequent, moderate, occasional, and non-attenders of Alcoholics Anonymous. *Journal of Clinical Psychology, 53*, 209–214.

Weber, R. (2000). *Principles of group psychotherapy*. New York, NY: American Group Psychotherapy Association.

Williams, P., Balabagno, A., Manahan, L., Piamjariyakul, U., Ranallo, L., Laurente, C., ... Williams, A. (2010). Symptom monitoring and self-care practices among Filipino cancer patients. *Cancer Nursing, 33*(1), 37–46.

Yalom, I. (1995). *The theory and practice of group psychotherapy* (4th ed.). New York, NY: Basic Books.

Yalom, I., & Leszcz. M. (2005). *The theory and practice of group psychotherapy* (5th ed.). New York, NY: Basic Books.

Index   • • • • •

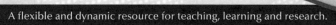